MARRIAGE:
AN ORTHODOX PERSPECTIVE

MARRIAGE:
AN ORTHODOX PERSPECTIVE

by
John Meyendorff

Professor of Patristics and Church History
and Dean
St. Vladimir's Orthodox Theological Seminary

Third revised edition

ST. VLADIMIR'S SEMINARY PRESS
CRESTWOOD, NEW YORK 10707
1984

by the same author

GREGORY PALAMAS: Defense of the Holy Hesychasts
  Text and French translation (1959; 2nd ed. 1974)
THE ORTHODOX CHURCH (1961; 2nd ed. 1981)
A STUDY OF GREGORY PALAMAS (1964)
ORTHODOXY AND CATHOLICITY (1966)
BYZANTINE THEOLOGY (1974)
ST. GREGORY PALAMAS AND ORTHODOX SPIRITUALITY
  (1974)
CHRIST IN EASTERN CHRISTIAN THOUGHT (1975)
BYZANTINE HESYCHASM: HISTORICAL, THEOLOGICAL
  AND SOCIAL PROBLEMS (1974)
CHRIST IN EASTERN CHRISTIAN THOUGHT (1975)
LIVING TRADITION (1978)
BYZANTIUM AND THE RISE OF RUSSIA (1980)
THE BYZANTINE LEGACY IN THE ORTHODOX CHURCH
  (1982)
CATHOLICITY AND THE CHURCH (1983)

First edition 1971
Revised edition 1975
Third revised edition 1984

Library of Congress Cataloging in Publication Data:
Meyendorff, Jean, 1926-
  Marriage.

1. Marriage.   I. Title.
HQ728.W43 1975   301.42   75-14241

MARRIAGE: AN ORTHODOX PERSPECTIVE

© Copyright 1975
by
ST. VLADIMIR'S SEMINARY PRESS

ALL RIGHTS RESERVED

ISBN 0-913836-05-2

PRINTED IN THE UNITED STATES OF AMERICA
BY
ATHENS PRINTING COMPANY
NEW YORK, N.Y.

Golden marriage ring—Constantinople; Dumbarton Oaks Collection, Washington, D. C. The Greek inscription reads: "Grace of God" and "Concord".

On the front cover:

Golden marriage belt, front medallion—Constantinople, VI or VII century; Dumbarton Oaks Collection, Washington, D. C. The Greek inscription reads: "From God, concord, grace and health."

Contents

MARRIAGE:
An Orthodox Perspective

INTRODUCTION

All Orthodox catechisms and textbooks define marriage as a *sacrament* or a "mystery" of the Church. At first glance, this definition may appear strange; marriage is practiced by Christians and non-Christians alike, by atheists, by generations of human beings who never heard what the word "sacrament" means. Man is born, gets married, begets children, and dies. These are the laws of nature which God established and blessed; but marriage particularly is singled out by the Church. The very special blessing which it bestows upon the man and the woman who get married is called a "sacrament." Why?

There is a very rich literature on marriage written by Roman Catholics and Protestants, by psychologists, psychoanalysts, sociologists, canonists. In our day and age mass media cultivate the issues connected with the sexual nature of man. They discuss publicly questions which the puritan generations of the past never envisaged even privately. It is being recognized widely that Freud and Jung revolutionized not only sexual ethics but also our very understanding of human nature. Meanwhile the Roman Catholic Church has also adopted attitudes which are difficult to justify, such as a total ban on "artificial" birth control (as if it were easy to establish a clear distinction between "artificial" and "natural" forms of contraception). In fact, the crisis created in the Roman Catholic world by the papal encyclical *Humanae vitae* involves much more than the issue of birth control; it presupposes a philosophy of marriage and marital responsibility. All this requires an Orthodox evaluation and response.

It is beyond the author's competence and the size of the present essay to discuss all the issues involving marriage and sexuality raised by the developments mentioned above. Our only topic is marriage as *sacrament,* i.e., an aspect which enters neither the field of psychology nor that of physiology nor that of sociology. It is the author's belief, however, that the Orthodox understanding of the *sacrament* of marriage suggests the only possible Christian attitude towards most of the issues raised today. This understanding is clearly different from those which traditionally prevailed in Western Christianity; and, thus, it may give different openings to practical solutions.

The very notion of marriage as a sacrament presupposes that man is not only a being with physiological, psychological, and social functions, but that he is a citizen of God's Kingdom, i.e., that his entire life—and especially its most decisive moments—involves *eternal values* and God Himself.

For Orthodox Christians, this essential involvement is best realized in the Eucharist. The Eucharist, or "Divine Liturgy," is the moment and the place when and where a Christian should realize what he truly is. In the Eucharist, the Kingdom of God—whose citizen he is by baptism—becomes available directly to his spiritual senses. The Divine Liturgy actually starts with the exclamation: "Blessed is the Kingdom of the Father and of the Son and of the Holy Spirit." In the Liturgy, the Church, being concretely a gathering of people, ceases to be a human organization and becomes truly the "Church of God." Then Christ Himself leads the assembly, and the assembly is transformed into His Body. Then all partitions between concrete historical happenings and eternity are broken. The true meaning of marriage as a sacrament becomes understandable in the framework of the Eucharistic Divine Liturgy.

In our contemporary practice the connection of marriage with the Eucharist is not obvious. Marriage appears to us primarily as a personal or a family affair. It may be blessed in Church and thus acquire a comforting flavor of both legitimacy and sacredness; but its relation to the Liturgy of the Church remains unclear for most of us. The actual church ceremony has no obvious relation to the Eucharist, and only a circle of invited relatives and friends take part in it. However, as we will try to show in this essay, it is impossible to understand either the New Testament doctrine on marriage, or the very consistent practice of the Orthodox Church, without seeing Christian marriage in the context of the Eucharist. The Eucharist, and the discipline which our communion in the Eucharist presupposes, is the key which explains the Christian attitude toward "church marriage" as well as toward those marriages which were or still are concluded outside the Church. Many practical difficulties which we face come from a misunderstanding of this basic connection of marriage with the Eucharist.

The misunderstanding must be corrected if we want to face our responsibilities in our modern, secular society, and if we desire an articulate Orthodox Christian answer to the challenges of the day. Actually, the "eucharistic" understanding of marriage clearly illustrates what is the essential Christian claim for man—an image of God, destined to participation in divine life itself. Psychologists and sociologists, on the basis of their respective limited fields of inquiry, may reach a foretaste of this truth, but certainly not affirm it in its entirety. The Christian experience of "God becoming man, so that man may become God" (St. Athanasius of Alexandria), is alone able to make the claim in all its daring significance. Of this, Christian marriage is also an expression.

The liturgical and historical facts mentioned in this essay are well known;[1] our task will consist only of drawing the

[1]See especially A. S. Pavlov, *Chapter Fifty of the Kormchaia Kniga,* Moscow, 1887 (in Russia) and S. V. Troitsky, *The Christian Philosophy of Marriage,* Paris, 1932 (in Russian); a brief survey in English in A. Smirensky, "The Evolution of the Present Rite of Matrimony and Parallel Developments" in *St. Vladimir's Seminary Quarterly,* 8, 1964, No. 1, pp. 38-48; cf. also Jean Dauvillier and Carlo de Clercq, *Le mariage en droit canonique oriental,* Paris, 1936; K. Ritzer, *Le mariage dans les Eglises chrétiennes,* Paris, Cerf, 1970; and T. Stylianopoulos, "Towards a Theology of Marriage in the Orthodox Church," *Greek Orthodox Theological Review* 22, 1977, pp. 249-283; R. Stephanopoulos, "Marriage and Family in Ecumenical Perspective," *St. Vladimir's Theological Quarterly* 25, 1981, pp. 21-34.

necessary conclusions and of trying to establish the pattern according to which the essential meaning of marriage can be brought again to the consciousness of Christians today.

I. JUDAISM AND THE NEW TESTAMENT

The Old Testament Judaic thought saw the essential meaning and goal of marriage in procreation. The most obvious and necessary sign of God's blessing was seen in the continuation of the race. Abraham's obedience and confidence in God brought the promise of a glorious posterity: "I will bless thee and in multiplying I will multiply thy seed as the stars of the heaven, and as the sand which is upon the sea shore; and thy seed shall possess the gate of his enemies; and in thy seed shall all the nations of the earth be blessed; because thou hast obeyed my voice" (Genesis 22:17-18). This solemn promise given to Abraham explains why the absence of children was seen as a curse, especially for women.

This view, so clearly reflected in the Old Testament, is originally connected to the fact that early Judaism did not have a clear notion of personal survival after death. At best one could hope for a shady and imperfect existence in a place called *sheol* (often inaccurately translated as "hell"). The Psalmist asks for God's help against his enemies who want to kill him; and he knows that God "remembers no more" the slain, who are "cut off from God's hand." Asking for God's help against those who want to kill him, he skeptically challenges God: "Wilt thou show wonders to the dead? Shall the dead arise and praise thee?" (Psalm 88:10). God was the "God of the living," and not of the dead. However, the promise to Abraham implied that life could be perpetuated through posterity, hence the central importance of childbirth.

If marriage—monogamous or polygamous—was the normal means, concubinage was also tolerated and even sometimes recommended to secure the continuation of the race (Genesis 16:1-3). The institution of the "levirate"

(Genesis 38:8) consisted of an obligation for a man to "raise the seed" of a dead brother by marrying his widow, and thus securing for him a partial survival in the children of his wife. Monogamous marriage, based on eternal love of a husband and a wife for each other, existed rather as an ideal image. It was implied in the story of creation, in the Song of Songs, in various prophetic images of the love of God for His people. But it never became an absolute religious norm or requirement.

In the New Testament, the meaning of marriage changes radically. The opposition is clear precisely because the texts use Old Testament categories of thought in order explicitly to modify them. Not a single New Testament text mentioning marriage points to procreation as its justification or goal. Childbirth itself is a means of salvation only if it is accomplished "in faith, love and sanctity" (I Tim. 2:15). Modification of Old Testament norms appears with particular clarity in three instances:

1) All three synoptic Gospels (Matthew 22:23-32; Mark 12:18-27; Luke 20:27-37) report Jesus' attitude towards the "levirate." It is important to notice that the question is related to Christ's teaching on resurrection and immortality, which cancels worries about survival through posterity. When the Sadducees ("which say that there is no resurrection") asked who, among the seven brothers who successively married the same woman, will have her to wife "in the resurrection," Jesus answers that "in the resurrection they neither marry, nor are given in marriage, but are as the angels of God in Heaven."

This text is often understood to imply that marriage is only an earthly institution and that its reality is dissolved by death. Such an understanding prevailed in the Western Church, which never discouraged remarriage of widowers and never limited the number of remarriages permitted to Christians. However, if this were the right understanding of Jesus' words, they would be in clear contradiction to the teaching of St. Paul and to the very consistent canonical practice of the Orthodox Church throughout the centuries. In the Christian understanding, marriage is absolutely unique and quite incompatible with the "levirate." Never would the Christian Church encourage a man to marry his brother's widow (see below, Chapter X). In fact, as Clement of Alexandria already noted, "The Lord is not rejecting marriage, but ridding their minds of the expectation that in the resurrection there will be carnal desire."[2] Jesus' answer to the Sadducees is strictly limited by the meaning of their question. They rejected the Resurrection because they could not understand it otherwise than as a restoration of earthly human existence, which would include the Judaic understanding of marriage as procreation through sexual intercourse. In this, Jesus says, they "err," because life in the Kingdom will be like that of the "angels." Jesus' answer is, therefore, nothing more than a denial of a naive and materialistic understanding of the Resurrection, and it does not give any positive meaning to marriage. He speaks of the *levirate,* and not of Christian marriage, whose meaning is revealed—implicitly and explicitly—in other parts of the New Testament.

2) Christ's teaching prohibiting divorce reflects, more positively, the nature of Christian marriage. It is expressed in direct opposition to the Jewish Deuteronomy, which allowed divorce (Matthew 5:32; 19:9; Mark 10:11; Luke 16:18). The very fact that Christian marriage is indissoluble excludes all utilitarian interpretations. The union between husband and wife is an end in itself; it is an eternal union between two unique and eternal personalities which cannot be broken by such concerns as "posterity" (the justification for concubinage) or family solidarity (the basis for the "levirate").

Indissolubility, however, is not a requirement which is *legally* absolute. The famous exception mentioned by Matthew ("save for the cause of fornication"—5:32) is there to remind us that the law of the Kingdom of God is never legally compelling, that it presupposes free human response, and that therefore the gift of Christian marriage needs to be accepted, freely lived, but can eventually be rejected by man. In general, the Gospel never reduces the mystery of human

---

[2]Clement of Alexandria (d. appr. 215 A.D.) is one of the founders of Christian theology. The quotation is from his Miscellanies, III, 12, 87, Engl. tr. in *The Library of Christian Classics,* II, Philadelphia, Pa., The Westminster Press, 1954, p. 81.

freedom to legal precepts. It offers man the only gift worthy of the "image of God"—"impossible" perfection. "Be perfect, as your Father is perfect." Christ's requirement of absolute monogamy also appeared as an impossibility to Christ's auditors (Matthew 19:10). In fact, love is beyond the categories of the possible and of the impossible. It is a "perfect gift," known only through experience. It is obviously incompatible with adultery. In case of adultery, the gift is refused, and marriage does not exist. What occurs then is not only legal "divorce," but a tragedy of misused freedom, i.e., of sin.

3) When he speaks of widowhood, St. Paul presupposes that marriage is not broken by death, for "love never fails" (Cor. 13:8). In general, Paul's attitude towards marriage is clearly distinct from the Jewish rabbinic view in that— especially in I Corinthians—he gives such strong preference to celibacy over marriage. Only in Ephesians is this negative view corrected by the doctrine of marriage as a reflection of the union between Christ and the Church—a doctrine which became the basis of the entire theology of marriage as found in Orthodox tradition.

However, on one issue—the remarriage of widowers— Paul's view, as it is expressed in I Corinthians, is strictly upheld by the canonical and sacramental tradition of the Church: "If they cannot contain, let them marry: for it is better to marry than to burn" (I Corinthians 7:9). Second marriage—either of a widower or of a divorcee—is only tolerated as better than "burning." Until the tenth century, it was not blessed in church and, even today, it remains an obstacle for entering the clergy. Our contemporary rite for blessing second marriages also shows clearly that it is admitted only by condescension. In any case, Scripture and Tradition agree that faithfulness of the widower or the widow to his or her deceased partner is more than an "ideal"; it is a Christian norm. Christian marriage is not only an earthly sexual union, but an eternal bond which will continue when our bodies will be "spiritual" and when Christ will be "all in all."

These three examples clearly show that in the New

Testament a totally new concept of marriage is being introduced; it is directly dependent upon the "Good News" of the
Resurrection which was brought by Christ. A Christian is
called—already in this world—to experience new life, to
become a citizen of the Kingdom; and he can do so in
marriage. But then marriage ceases to be either a simple
satisfaction of temporary natural urges, or a means for
securing an illusory survival through posterity. It is a unique
union of two beings in love, two beings who can transcend
their own humanity and thus be united not only "with each
other," but also "in Christ."

II. THE EARLY CHURCH AND ROMAN LAW

In the Roman world, marriage was not conceived primarily
as a means to secure posterity but as an agreement between
two freely-choosing parties. The famous principle of Roman
law, specifying that "marriage is not in the intercourse, but
in the consent" (*nuptias non concubitus, sed consensus facit*),
and the definition popularized by Modestinus that "cohabitation with a free woman is marriage, and not concubinage"—
which presupposed that a slave woman could not give her
free consent, and that, therefore, cohabitation with her could
never be called "marriage"—are the very basis of civil law in
all modern civilized countries. The essence of marriage lies
in the consent which, in turn, gives meaning and legal
substance to the marriage *agreement,* or *contract.*

The fact that marriage was conceived, in Roman law, as
an agreement between two free parties implied a substantial
social progress if compared to the concepts prevailing in
other ancient civilizations. It provided the legal framework
for the total emancipation of women and their legal equality
to men.

As a legal contract, whose subjects were only the parties
involved, marriage did not need any third party to give it
legal validity. The State, however, provided facilities for the

registration of marriage agreements. Registration implied control over their conformity with the laws and provided ready material for the courts, when the latter were to rule on conflicts connected with individual marriages.

Just as the Mosaic Law, Roman Law provided for the possibility of dissolving marriage contracts. The conditions of divorce varied greatly both before and after the Christian era.

The Christian Church, both at the time of persecution and during her alliance with the Roman State, accepted the Roman laws regulating marriage. Even when Christianity became the prevailing State religion, the ancient definitions of marriage as "contract" continued to be accepted in State laws and even in the ecclesiastical *Nomocanon in Fourteen Titles.* It is also found in the Slavic version of the *Nomocanon,* the so-called *Kormchaia Kniga* ("Book of the Rudder")[3] which was the foundation of canon law in Slavic countries until the beginning of the nineteenth century.

The same conformity with Roman concepts and terminology is found in the writings of the early Fathers. The following are the words of the second-century writer Athenagoras in his *Apology* to Emperor Marcus Aurelius (Chapter 33): "Everyone of us considers as his the woman whom he married *according to your laws.*" St. John Chrysostom (d. 404) refers directly to "civil law" when he defines marriage as "nothing else than closeness, or affinity" (*Hom. 56 on Genesis,* 2).

The number of patristic quotations on this issue can easily be multiplied. Their meaning, however, is not that the Church was indifferent to the issue of marriage, nor that she had no specific point of view and simply adopted as her own the prevailing Roman concept of marriage as contract. The following chapters will show that the contrary is true. Never, in her entire history, did the Christian Church show more clearly that she was bringing into the world a new and unprecedented divine reality and presence. And the New Testament texts quoted above show that this new reality also implied a

---

[3]Not to be confused with the Greek "Rudder," or *Pedalion,* a canonical compilation of the eighteenth century, which is also available in English.

completely new attitude towards marriage, different from both the Judaic and the Roman concepts. This new reality was not originally expressed in any specific and independent marriage ritual, and its nature did not consist in suppressing the laws which secular society had set. Christians understood the value of the Roman order. They appreciated the progress which some aspects of Roman Law were introducing in human relations. But while accepting all that, they never forgot the specific and totally new experience and commitment which they accepted in Baptism and the Eucharist. What mattered, therefore, was not the particular ceremony used to conclude the marriage, but *who* was accepting the marriage contract. If the parties were Christian, their marriage was a Christian marriage, involving Christian responsibility and Christian experience. For them, marriage was a sacrament, not simply a legal agreement.

III. MARRIAGE AS SACRAMENT OR "MYSTERY"

"This is a great mystery: but I speak concerning Christ and the Church" (Ephesians 5:32). In chapter 5 of the letter to the Ephesians we discover the *different* meaning of Christian marriage, that element which cannot be reduced to either Judaic utilitarianism or Roman legalism—the possibility and the responsibility given to both husband and wife to transfigure their "agreement" into the reality of the Kingdom.

Every human being is a member of earthly society, a citizen of his country, and a member of his family. He cannot avoid the needs of material existence and must fulfill his social obligations. The Gospel does not deny man's responsibility for the world and for human society. True Christianity never called for a denial of the world. Even monks render a peculiar service to the world by denying not its existence and its importance, but its claims to control man and to restrict his freedom. The calling of man—the "image and likeness of God" in him—is, first of all, a limitless, a "divine," a free use of his creative potentials, his yearning for the absolute Good, for the highest forms of Beauty, for true Love, for the posibility of really *experiencing* this Goodness; because God Himself is that Goodness, that Beauty, that Love and He Himself loves man. To Him man can appeal; His voice he can hear and His love he can experience. For a Christian, God is not an idea to be understood, but a Person to meet: "I am in my Father, and you are in Me and I am in you" (John 14:20). In God man discovers his own humanity, because he has been created as an "image of God." And Christ, being True God, also manifested a true humanity, not in spite of His divinity, but precisely *because* He was True God: in Him, we see divinity as the true norm of humanity.

When man is baptized and becomes "one body" with Christ in the Eucharist, he, in fact, becomes more fully himself; he recovers a truer relationship with God and with fellow-men, and he returns to his worldly responsibilities with all the God-given and limitless potential of creativity, of service, and of love.

Now, if St. Paul calls marriage a "mystery" (or "sacrament": the Greek word is the same), he means that in marriage man does not only satisfy the needs of his earthly, secular existence, but also realizes something very important of the purpose for which he was created; i.e., he enters the realm of eternal life. In the world, man does possess a diversity of talents and powers—material, intellectual, emotional—but his existence is limited by *time.* Now, to "be born from the water and the Spirit" is to enter the realm of eternal life; for through Christ's Resurrection this realm is already open and can be experienced and shared. By calling marriage a "mystery," St. Paul affirms that marriage also has a place in the eternal Kingdom. The husband becomes one single being, one single "flesh" with his wife, just as the Son of God ceased to be only Himself, i.e., God, and became *also* man so that the community of His people may also become His Body. This is why, so often, the Gospel narratives compare the Kingdom of God with a wedding feast, which fulfills the Old Testament prophetic visions of a wedding between God and Israel, the elected people. And this is also why a truly Christian marriage can only be unique, not in virtue of some abstract law or ethical precept, but precisely because it is a Mystery of the Kingdom of God introducing man into *eternal* joy and *eternal* love.

As a mystery, or sacrament, Christian marriage certainly conflicts with the practical, empirical reality of "fallen" humanity. It appears, just as the Gospel itself, as an unattainable ideal. But there is a crucial difference between a "sacrament" and an "ideal." A sacrament is not an imaginary abstraction. It is an experience where man is not involved alone, but where he acts in communion with God. In a sacrament, humanity participates in the higher reality of the Spirit, without, however, ceasing to be fully humanity. Actually, as we have said above, it becomes more authentically human and fulfills its original destiny. A sacrament is a "passage" to true life; it is man's salvation. It is an open door into true, unadulterated humanity.

A sacrament, therefore, *is not magic.* The Holy Spirit does not suppress human freedom but, rather, liberates man from the limitations of sinfulness. In the new life, the impossible becomes truly possible, if only man freely accepts what God gives. This applies to marriage as well.

Mistakes, misunderstandings, and even conscious rebellion against God, i.e., sin, are possible as long as man lives in the present empirical and visible existence of the "fallen world." The Church understands this very well, and this is why the "mystery" of the Kingdom revealed in marriage is not reduced in Orthodox practice to a set of legal rules. But true understanding and justified condescension to human weakness are possible only if one recognizes the absolute norm of the New Testamental doctrine of marriage as sacrament.

IV. MARRIAGE AND EUCHARIST

If, as we have seen above, marriage was conceived by the Early Church as a "sacrament," anticipating the joy of the

Kingdom of God, how can we explain the fact that this Church did not use any particular ceremony, or rite, to sanction marriage? Instead, it recognized as normal a marriage concluded according to the laws of secular society. It never tried to abolish these laws nor to destroy the social order which instituted them.

The answer to this question is that the difference between a non-Christian and a Christian marriage lies in the fact that the first was concluded between two pagans while the second involved two Christians; it did not lie in the manner in which it was concluded. One of the constant reminders of St. Paul was that God did not live in "man-made temples," and that "our bodies are the temple of the Holy Spirit." When in marriage a man and a woman become "one flesh," and if both are members of the Body of Christ, their union is being sealed by the Holy Spirit living in each of them.

Now *the Eucharist* is what makes them members of the Body of Christ.

The connection between marriage and the Eucharist is alluded to in the story of the marriage in Cana (John 2:1-11), the reading adopted during our contemporary rite of "crowning." This text is one of the numerous texts of the Johannine Gospel pointing at Baptism and the Eucharist:[4] as water is transformed into wine, so the sinful life of man can be transfigured, by the presence of Christ, into the new reality of the Kingdom.

Early Christian writers—the same ones who otherwise give full recognition to the legal validity of civil marriage "according to laws"—also affirm that it is the Eucharist which gives to marriage its specifically Christian meaning. Thus Tertullian (second century) writes that marriage "is arranged by the church, confirmed by the oblation (the Eucharist), sealed by the blessing, and inscribed in heaven by the angels" (*To His Wife, II,* 8:6-9). Every Christian couple desirous of marriage went through the formalities of civil registration, which gave it validity in secular society; and then through their joint participation in the regular Sunday liturgy, in the presence of the entire local Christian com-

[4]Cf. O. Cullmann, *Early Christian Worship,* Napierville, Ill., 1956.

munity, they received the Bishop's blessing. It was then that their civil agreement became also "sacrament," with eternal value, transcending their earthly lives because it was also "inscribed in heaven," and not only in a secular "registry." It became an eternal union in Christ. The same procedure is implied in a letter of the famous bishop-martyr Ignatius of Antioch (ca. 100 A.D.): "Those who get married must unite with the knowledge of the bishop, so that marriage may be according to the Lord, and not by human desire" (*To Polycarp*, 5:2).

What makes a "sacrament" is not necessarily a set of specific, visible gestures, accomplished by a valid minister. Actually, the Church itself—a mysterious union of God with His people—is the Sacrament, the Mystery of salvation (cf. esp. Ephesians 3). When man is incorporated into this union through Baptism, this is indeed "sacrament," for the Mystery of salvation is applied to the individual commitment of that man. But all these individual "sacraments" are "completed" in the Eucharist, as we read in Nicholas Cabasilas, the great Orthodox mystic and theologian of the fourteenth century (*On the Life in Christ*, PG 150, col. 585B). Actually the Eucharist is itself a wedding feast, so often mentioned in the Gospels, as Cabasilas also writes: "This is the most-praised wedding, to which the Bridegroom leads the Church as a Virgin bride . . . when we become flesh of His flesh and bones of His bones" (*ibid.*, col. 593D).

Baptism, in the Early Church, was celebrated during the Liturgy, and so are, even today, the services of ordination to the diaconate, the priesthood, and the episcopate. This was originally the case with marriage. Only this understanding of Christian marriage as an integral part of the Mystery, of which the Eucharist is the "completion," can explain the canonical regulations against "mixed marriages," against "second marriages," etc., as we shall see below. These marriages could not be fully sacramental. Perfectly "legitimate" in terms of civil law, they could not be integrated into the Eucharist.

Many confusions and misunderstandings concerning marriage in our contemporary Orthodox practice would be easily eliminated if the original connection between marriage and the Eucharist were restored. Theoretically, Orthodox sacramental theology—even in its scholastic, "textbook" form—has preserved this connection in affirming, in opposition to Roman Catholicism, that the priest is the "minister" of marriage.[5] Western medieval theology, on the contrary, has created a series of confusions by adopting—as in so many other points—Roman legalism as the basis of sacramental theology: marriage, being a "contract," is concluded by the husband and wife themselves, who are therefore the "ministers" of the sacrament, the priest being only a witness. As a legal contract, marriage is dissolved by the death of one of the partners, but it is indissoluble as long as both are alive. Actually, indissolubility—i.e., a legal concept taken as an absolute—is the main, if not the only, contribution of Christianity to the Roman Catholic concept of marriage. Broken by death, assimilated with a human agreement, marriage, in the prevailing Western view, is only an earthly affair, concerned with the "body," unworthy of entering the Kingdom of God. One can even wonder whether marriage, so understood, can still be called a sacrament. But, by affirming that the priest is the minister of the marriage, as he is also the minister of the Eucharist, the Orthodox Church implicitly integrates marriage in the *eternal* Mystery, where the boundaries between heaven and earth are broken and where human decision and action acquire an eternal dimension.

Paradoxically, however, the Roman Catholic Church has preserved the ancient Christian tradition in its liturgical discipline; a marriage between two Roman Catholics still occurs in connection with a mass. The latter is omitted, however, in cases of mixed marriages. A restoration of a similar discipline in the Orthodox Church would certainly fit the Orthodox theology of marriage better than it does the legal concepts which prevailed in Roman Catholicism at a

[5]P. Trembelas, *Dogmatique de l'Eglise Catholique Orthodoxe*, III, Chevetogne, 1968, p. 364; T. Stylianopoulos, "Towards a Theology of Marriage in the Orthodox Church," *Greek Orthodox Theological Review* 22, 1977, pp. 249-283; R. Stephanopoulos, "Marriage and Family in Ecumenical Perspective," *St. Vladimir's Theological Quarterly* 25, 1981, pp. 21-34.

time when Roman Catholic theology ceased to view its own traditional liturgy as a source of its theology!

In some extreme situations, the Orthodox Church is, even today, forced into the position it held during the first centuries. In the Soviet Union, for example—where the celebration of church "crowning" is often unfeasible because of State persecution of religion, but where an anonymous reception of the Eucharist is possible without drawing the attention of authorities—the Church can and does, in fact, tolerate the marriages of Christians even without a formal Church ceremony. Due to the circumstances, this toleration is legitimate. It would, of course, be perfectly inadmissible wherever the Church has the possibility to perform the solemn office of crowning. And, in any case, admission to the Eucharist always implies that the Church knows that a given couple is not only married legitimately, from the Christian point of view, but also intends to live in accordance with the Gospel. The same logic also applies to a non-Orthodox couple who join the Church. Baptized if necessary, or only chrismated, or simply presenting their Confession of Orthodox faith, they are not "remarried," because their acceptance to the Eucharist implies that the Church blesses them as husband and wife.[6] The practice of "remarrying" such couples can be due only to a complete misunderstanding of the Orthodox doctrine of marriage.

V. WEDDING AS A SEPARATE RITE

Until the ninth century the Church did not know any rite of marriage separate from the eucharistic Liturgy.[7] Normally, after entering a civil marriage, the Christian couple partook

[6]Cf. Jerome Kotsonis (former Archbishop of Athens), Ἡ κανονικὴ ἄποψις περὶ τῆς ἐπικοινωνίας μετὰ τῶν ἑτεροδόξων, Athens, 1957, p. 216, and also the decisions of the Russian Holy Synod concerning the matter quoted in P. I. Nechaev, *Prakticheskoe rukovodstvo dlia sviashchenno-sluzhitelei*, 9th edition, St. Petersburg, 1907, p. 263-264.

[7]Cf. for example A. Zavialov, *Brak* ("Marriage"), article in the

of the Eucharist, and this communion was—according to Tertullian—the seal of marriage, implying all the Christian responsibilities which we discussed above.

However, since the fourth century a specific solemnization of the sacrament is mentioned by Eastern Christian writers: a rite of "crowning," performed during the eucharistic Liturgy. According to St. John Chrysostom, the crowns symbolized victory over "passions," for Christian marriage—a sacrament of eternity—was not concluded "according to the flesh." From a letter of St. Theodore Studite (d. 826) we learn that crowning was accompanied by a brief prayer read "before the whole people" at the Sunday Liturgy, by the bishop or the priest. The text of the prayer, given by St. Theodore, is the following: "Thyself, O Master, send down Thy hand from Thy holy dwelling place and unite these Thy servant and Thy handmaid. And give to those whom Thou unitest harmony of minds; crown them into one flesh; make their marriage honorable; keep their bed undefiled; deign to make their common life blameless" (Letters I, 22, PG 99, col. 973). The liturgical books of the same period (such as the famous *Codex Barberini*) contain several short prayers similar to that quoted by St. Theodore. These prayers are all meant to be read during the Liturgy.[8]

The appearance of this brief rite of crowning does not mean, however, that it immediately became required for all Christians contracting marriage. The well-known legal collection, known as *Epanagoge,* describing in detail the relations between Church and State—and whose author is most probably the great patriarch Photius (857-867, 877-886)— still offers to Christians three alternatives for concluding marriage: "Marriage," writes Photius, "is an alliance between husband and wife and their union for their entire life; it is accomplished by a blessing, or by a crowning, or by an agreement" (XVI, 1). From the sixth to the ninth centuries, imperial state legislation tended to grant the Church an ever increasing control over marriages (see, for example, novella

Orthodox Theological Encyclopedia (in Russian), A. P. Lopukhin, ed., vol. II, Petrograd, 1903, pp. 1029-1030, 1034.

[8]See Goar, *Euchologion,* repr. Graz, 1960, pp. 321-322.

64 of Justinian), but it never made "crowning" a legal obligation.

The decisive step in this direction was taken at the beginning of the tenth century, and this measure coincided with the appearance of a rite of crowning *separate* from the Eucharist. What provided this change which modified fundamentally, if not the meaning of marriage, at least its understanding by the vast majority of faithful?

The answer can easily be found in the imperial decree which enforced the change. In his novella 89 (novella: "new law") the Byzantine Emperor Leo VI (d. 912) first expresses regrets that in previous imperial legislation the two legal acts of adoption of a child and of marriage were considered as purely civil formalities. He then declares that both of these acts—as long as they involve free citizens, and not slaves—will henceforth be sanctioned by a Church ceremony. A marriage not blessed by the Church "will not be considered as marriage," but as an illegitimate concubinage.[9]

Several aspects of this text deserve attention—for example, the parallel between the act of marriage and that of adoption of children,[10] and the fact that slaves are not covered by the new law. But the most important implication of the decree is that the Church is invested with the responsibility of giving *legal status* to marriage. In spite of the very close connection between Church and State which existed during the ninth century in all the Christian countries, such a responsibility was quite unusual for the Church. The change was indeed striking. Before Leo VI a citizen could enter a marriage disapproved by the Church (second or third marriage, mixed marriage, etc.), and do so legally. If he was a Christian, his action incurred a period of penitence and excommunication (as we will see below), but he remained in good standing before the law. After Leo VI the Church had to determine the legal status of all marriages, even those which contradicted Christian norms. Of course the new situation, in principle, gave the Church an upper hand over the morals

[9]A. Dain, *Les Novelles de Leon VI, le Sage,* Paris, 1944, pp. 294-297 (Greek text and French translation), Eng. tr. below, p. 109.

[10]Would it not be desirable, even today, to give a religious significance to adoption?

of all citizens; but in practice, since these citizens were not all saints, the Church was obliged not only to bless marriages which it did not approve, but even to "dissolve" them (i.e., give "divorces"). The distinction between the "secular" and the "sacred," between fallen human society and the Kingdom of God, between marriage as contract and marriage as sacrament, was partially obliterated.

The Church had to pay a high price for the new social responsibility which it had received; it had to "secularize" its pastoral attitude towards marriage and practically abandon its penitential discipline. Was it possible, for example, to refuse Church blessing to a remarried widower when this refusal implied deprivation of civil rights for one or two years? As soon as the sacrament of marriage—received in the Church— became legally obligatory, compromises of all sorts became unavoidable; and, simultaneously, the idea that marriage was a unique and eternal bond—reflecting the union of Christ and the Church—was obliterated in the pastoral practice of the Church and in the conscience of the faithful. Emperor Leo VI himself, the author of the novella, forced upon the Church his own *fourth* marriage with Zoe Carbonopsina in 906.

The only compromise which the Church could not accept, however, was to mitigate the holiness of the Eucharist: it could not, for example, give communion to a non-Orthodox, or to a couple entering a second marriage. Thus, it had to develop a rite of marriage separate from the Eucharist. The change was made more acceptable by the fact that the obvious connection between Church marriage and Eucharist was lost anyway as soon as Church marriage became a *legal* requirement.

However, even the novella of Leo VI failed to suppress entirely the possibility for a particular category of Church members to marry sacramentally, through the Eucharist, without a separate—and often expensive—"crowning." The slaves, i.e., more than half of the Empire's population, were not touched by the new law. This discrepancy between marriage law for slaves and for free citizens was suppressed by Emperor Alexis I Comnenos (1081-1118) who issued another novella making "crowning" a legal obligation for slaves as well.

By establishing a rite of "crowning" separate from the Eucharist, the Church did not forget, however, the original and normal link between marriage and Eucharist. This is clearly shown in the text by St. Symeon of Thessalonica quoted below (Appendix IV). Ancient forms of the rite include communion of the bridal pair—the rubric says: "if they are worthy"—with the reserved Sacrament. Communion was then preceded with the priest's exclamation: "The presanctified Holy Things for the holy!" and accompanied by the communion hymn: "I will receive the cup of the Lord."[11] A marriage rite including communion with reserved Sacrament was used in the Church as late as the fifteenth century: it is found in Greek manuscript service books of the thirteenth and in the Slavic books until the fifteenth.[12] In cases where the married couple was not "worthy"—i.e., when the marriage was not in conformity with Church norms—they partook not of the Sacrament, but only of a common cup of wine blessed by the priest. This practice—similar to the distribution of blessed bread, or *antidoron* at the end of the Liturgy to those who are not "worthy" of communion—became universal and is still adopted today. But even our contemporary rite preserves several features witnessing to its original connection with the Eucharist. It starts, as the Liturgy does, with the exclamation: "Blessed is the Kingdom of the Father and of the Son and of the Holy Spirit," and partaking of the common cup is preceded by the singing of the Lord's Prayer, as is communion during the Eucharistic liturgy.

In its canonical and practical tradition, the Church also remembered the fact that the Eucharist is the true "seal" of marriage. Marriages concluded before Baptism, i.e., without

[11]Cf. an euchologion of the tenth century found in the library of Mount Sinai; text in A.A. Dmitrievsky, *Opisanie Liturgicheskikh Rukopisei*, II, Εὐχολόγια, Kiev, 1901, p. 31. It is the practice in Greek churches, even today, to sing the communion hymn at the moment of the common cup.

[12]A. Katansky, "Towards a History of the Marriage Rite" (in Russian), in *Khristianskoe Chtenie*, St. Petersburg, 1880, I, pp. 112, 116.

connection to the Liturgy, have no sacramental meaning.[13] A newly baptized Christian can enter a second marriage with a Christian woman and then be admitted as a candidate for ordination to the priesthood as if he had been married only once (Apostolic canon 17). On the other hand, as we saw above, a non-Christian couple admitted into the Church through Baptism, Chrismation, and Communion is not "re-married"; their joint reception of the Eucharist is the Christian fulfillment of a "natural" marriage concluded outside the Church.

In our time the connection between marriage and the Eucharist must—and can easily be—restored again. What better way does the Church have to show to its children the true sacramental meaning of the act they are accomplishing?

VI. THE CONTEMPORARY RITE OF BETROTHAL

The new responsibility given to the Church by the laws of Emperors Leo VI and Alexis I—that of giving formal legitimacy to all marriages—required the adoption of new liturgical forms. These new forms, on the one hand, were to be separate from the Eucharist and, on the other hand, had to reflect the eternal and unchangeable teachings of the Church about the meaning of marriage. Orthodox Byzantium, with its remarkable ability to interpret Scripture, to relate it to the central mystery of Christ, to use signs and symbols in expressing the meaning of the Christian faith, produced in the tenth and eleventh centuries the two present-day Orthodox services of betrothal and crowning.

Today, the service of betrothal generally immediately precedes the crowning. It is celebrated in the back of the church (technically, in the narthex or vestibule) and is

---

[13]The opposite opinion, expressed by S. V. Troitsky in his otherwise very valuable book on *The Christian Philosophy of Marriage,* seems to lack theological or canonical basis.

followed by a solemn procession of the bridal pair towards the ambo, where the crowning service follows. Characteristically, however, the Church keeps the two services, at least in principle, distinct; and they can be celebrated separately. Each corresponds to a distinct aspect of marriage. The betrothal service is the new form of a marriage *contract*, with the bridegroom and bride pledging mutual faithfulness. It was originally a civil ceremony. By assuming responsibility for it, the Church did not suppress the legal and moral obligations imposed by the Old Testament law, by Roman law and still maintained by our own contemporary society. She rather provided them with a new Biblical and spiritual meaning.

After an initial Great Litany, which includes special petitions for the bridal pair, the service is composed of two short prayers, of an exchange of rings, and of a longer concluding prayer. For the man and the woman of today, it is not always easy to catch the true meaning and relevance of Biblical events referred to in the text of the prayers. However, even a superficial familiarity with the Bible, interpreted in the light of Christ, leads immediately to a remarkably consistent vision.

We have seen in Chapter III that the images used in the New Testament to describe the Kingdom of God see Christ as the *bridegroom* of saved mankind, and His coming as a wedding feast. Liberated from spiritual barrenness and united with Christ, humanity acquires the fertility of the Spirit. It becomes the "Church of God," whose children are not born to death, but to life and immortality. The *mystery* of marriage allows for a similar life-giving union on the human level, in the love between a man and a woman.

The two short prayers—probably the most ancient ones—of the service of betrothal associate marriage with the saving work of Christ, who restores the unity between God and fallen mankind, by "espousing" human nature. The text uses the Old Testament example of the marriage between Isaac, the heir of Abraham, and Rebecca, the bride from distant Mesopotamia:

O eternal God, who hast brought into unity those who
were sundered, and hast ordained for them an indissoluble
bond of love, who didst bless Isaac and Rebecca, and
didst make them heirs of Thy promise: Bless also these Thy
servants, _____ and _____, guiding them unto
every good work. . . .

O Lord our God, who hast espoused the Church as a pure
virgin from among the gentiles: Bless this betrothal, and
unite and maintain these Thy servants in peace and oneness
of mind. . . .

The account of the betrothal of Isaac and Rebecca (Gen.
24)—one of the most beautiful stories preserved in the book
of Genesis—comes out again at the beginning of the last and
longer prayer which follows the exchange of rings:

O Lord our God, who didst accompany the servant of the
patriarch Abraham into Mesopotamia, when he was sent
to espouse a wife for his lord Isaac, and who, by means
of the drawing of water, didst reveal to him that he should
betroth Rebecca: Do Thou, the same Lord, bless also the
betrothal of these Thy servants . . .

Although Rebecca, the daughter of Abraham's brother
Nahor (Gen. 22:22), was a close relative of Isaac and
the mission of the servant Eliezer to bring her as his bride
was motivated by Abraham's desire not to see Isaac find a
pagan "Canaanite" wife (Gen. 24:3), her coming required
a mission to a far country, where Abraham used to live as
a nomad among the Aramaeans.

This is the reason why the Fathers of the Church saw in
Isaac's and Rebecca's betrothal a "type" of the call of the
Gentiles to Christ. The Fathers also saw a figure of Baptism
in the fact that Rebecca was identified by the servant Eliezer
when she drew *water* out of the well (Gen. 24:14): so also
baptism through water reconciles mankind with God. Each
Christian soul is betrothed to Christ by rising from the
baptismal font.

This interpretation of the story is adopted by the betrothal
prayers, which also mention the "unity" of the "sundered"
parts of creation, the "calling" of the Church from among
the Gentiles and recall that Rebecca was invited to become

Isaac's bride when she drew water from the well. This invitation to Rebecca was just the beginning of her life with Isaac, just as baptism is only the beginning of Christian life. So the betrothal prayer inaugurates a life in common which still lies ahead, just as the apostolic call to the Gentiles begins a long history of Christ's Church. But the ultimate goal is always the same: the restoration of lost unity with God, the reintegration of human life into its authentic wholeness. This is also the meaning of a Christian betrothal.

However, reintegration of mankind through love cannot withstand the powers of division and sin without God's *faithfulness* to His promise. The theme of faithfulness is thus the main one in the betrothal service and is expressed in the symbolism of the *rings*.

We are generally accustomed to interpret the exchange of rings simply as a pledge of mutual faithfulness. Secular society itself has widely accepted the custom. It is noteworthy, however, that none of the four Biblical references used in the "prayer of the rings" interprets the rite in this limited and merely human sense. In all the references, the ring is a sign of *God's pledge* to man (not necessarily in connection with marriage): Joseph received a ring from the pharaoh of Egypt as a sign of his new power (Gen. 41:42); the king of Babylon, with his ring, sealed the lions' den where Daniel was being thrown, as a pledge of his faithfulness to the suffering prophet, a faithfulness which God endorsed by saving Daniel from the lions (Dan. 6:17); Tamar, before giving herself to Judah, asked for his ring as a pledge of safety so that on the day she would be brought to trial before the same Judah, the ring would save her from the punishment due to harlots (Gen. 38:18); finally, in the parable of the prodigal son, the ring is a sign of the father's regained favor for his lost son (Luke 15:22).

To these four examples concerning the rings, the prayer adds the symbolism of the *right hand*: Moses' right hand was, in fact, God's hand, which brought the waters of the Red Sea over the Egyptians (Exodus 15:26) and which is, in fact, nothing other than the power of God, "making firm" the foundations of the earth.

Is, then, the betrothal a simple legal agreement between two parties? Can one of them break it at will? Not if the Church of God is called to be the contract's witness. For in that case, God Himself pledges His blessing and support, and unfaithfulness to each other means, for Christians, a betrayal of God and a rejection of His promise to grant them a new integrated and wholesome life.

So the betrothal service is the marriage contract as the Church understands it. It involves not only the bridal pair, but God Himself. This is the reason why canon 98 of the Sixth Ecumenical Council stipulates:

> He who brings to the intercourse of marriage a woman who is betrothed to another man, who is still alive, is to lie under the charge of adultery.

Byzantine canonists who wrote interpretations of this canon emphasize that betrothal and marriage are *legally* identical. One of them, Theodore Balsamon, even refers to the example of St. Joseph and the Virgin Mary, who were only betrothed to each other: still the Angel called Mary Joseph's "wife" (Matthew 1:20). This explains why, when the Church took charge of divorce procedures, these had to be followed also by a couple who were not yet "married" but only betrothed. The novella of Emperor Alexis I Comnenos (1081-1118), which, as we have already seen, had universalized the Church's competence in marital affairs, stated that betrothal could be broken only through formal divorce.

Thus a betrothal, solemnly celebrated in Church, is more than a simple "engagement." It represents the real bond of marriage, lacking only the ultimate sacramental fulfilment. This is certainly why it is generally celebrated just before the crowning service itself.

VII. THE CROWNING

In solemn procession, led by the priest, the bridegroom and bride enter the middle of church, welcomed by the singing of Psalm 128 (127). Each verse of the psalm is accompanied by a refrain: "Glory to Thee, our God, glory to Thee."

> Blessed is every one who fears the Lord, who walks in his
>   ways!
> You shall eat the fruit of the labor of your hands;
>   you shall be happy, and it shall be well with you.
> Your wife will be like a fruitful vine within your house;
>   your children will be like olive shoots around your table.
> Lo, thus shall the man be blessed who fears the Lord.
> The Lord bless you from Zion!
>   May you see the prosperity of Jerusalem
>   all the days of your life!
> May you see your children's children!
>   Peace be upon Israel!

This psalm belonged already to the liturgy of the Old Testament temple in Jerusalem. It was one of the "hymns of degrees," sung on the steps of the temple, when the levites were entering the sanctuary on solemn feast days. It exalts the joy of family life, the prosperity and peace which it brings to man as the highest forms of God's blessing.

However, when psalms are used in the Church of the New Testament, they also acquire a *new* meaning: "Zion" is the "Temple of the body of Christ" (John 2:2); "Jerusalem" is the eternal city "descending out of heaven from God" (Rev. 20:10); "Israel" is the new people of God, united in His Church. The procession before the crowning signifies therefore, an entrance into the Kingdom of Christ: the marriage contract concluded through the betrothal service will now be transformed into an eternal relationship; human love will acquire a totally new dimension by being identified with the love of Christ for His Church. The crowning service will now begin with a solemn proclamation by the priest: "Blessed is the Kingdom of the Father, and of the Son, and of the Holy Spirit."

Immediately after the procession, and as something of an anticlimax, the Slavic editions of the *Euchologion* (Service Book) require that the priest question the bridegroom and the bride:

Do you, _____, have a good, free and unconstrained will and a firm intention to take as your wife (or husband) this woman (or man), _____, whom you see here before you?

Have you promised yourself to any other bride (or man)?

These questions, which are not a part of the original Orthodox crowning service and which do not exist in the Greek *Euchologia,* were introduced in the famous *Trebnik* of the Metropolitan of Kiev, Peter Moghila (seventeenth century). Kiev found itself then within the borders of the Polish kingdom, and the questions are directly inspired by the Latin marriage rite, where the "consent" of the bridal pair is seen as the essential "formula" of marriage, whose "ministers" are the bridegroom and the bride themselves. Mutual "consent" was also a requirement of Polish law, giving validity to a marriage ceremony. In Orthodoxy, however, as was shown above, the meaning of the marriage crowning is to integrate the bridal pair into the very Mystery of Christ's love for the Church: their "consent" is doubtlessly required as a condition, but it is not the very *content* of the sacrament. The questions asked by the priest of the bridegroom and bride and their positive answers must be seen as a useful way of emphasizing their personal commitment and active participation in the celebration of the sacrament, but they would certainly be more appropriately asked during the betrothal service, together with the mutual pledge and the exchange of rings, than at the solemn beginning of the crowning service itself.

Originally celebrated in the framework of the Eucharistic liturgy, the crowning service is composed of the following five major elements:

1. The prayers.
2. The imposition of the crowns.
3. The Scripture readings.
4. The Lord's Prayer and the common cup.
5. The circular procession, sometimes designated as the "dance of Isaiah."

All couples intending to get married should make a point of reading the entire service carefully in advance, not only in terms of ceremonial rehearsal, but primarily for the sake of conscious and prayerful participation. The following brief remarks on each of these five parts are intended not as a full interpretation of the service but only as basic guidelines:

1. Our general lack of familiarity with the Bible, and particularly with the Old Testament, explains the question so frequently asked: why do the prayers of the crowning service mention so many personalities of Biblical history? The answer lies in the fact that marriage implies faithfulness, and the Biblical personalities and episodes enumerated in the prayers affirm the first and foremost truth: that God remains faithful to His people in spite of all historical vicissitudes and human sins, as long as man has faith in God. The genealogy of Christ, going back to Abraham as reported by St. Matthew (1:1-16), or to Adam, as we find it in St. Luke (3:23-38), witnesses to the fact that the chain of generations *was leading to a goal*: the coming of Christ, the Messiah; that, in the framework of God's plan for mankind's history, human fertility was a means for bringing man back to God; that, therefore, in Biblical history, marriage was not only a function determined by either sociological or physiological appetites but was leading to a point when God "from the root of Jesse according to the flesh, didst bud forth the ever-virgin one and wast incarnate of her and wast born of her for the redemption of the human race" (first prayer of the crowning service).

God Himself becoming man: this is the goal of Israel's history and the reason why God blessed Abraham and Sarah, Isaac and Rebecca, Jacob and Rachel, Joseph and Aseneth, Zechariah and Elizabeth, Joachim and Anna.

The first long prayer of the crowning service asks God to place the bridegroom and the bride in the company of these holy couples, the ancestors of Christ, to bestow upon them the same blessing. Certainly in a sense the Kingdom of God has already been revealed, and it will not result from any future historical event; but all children of Christian couples are called to become "members of Christ," participants in His Body. Each one of them, in his or her particular personal way, is called to experience the presence of God and to reveal Him to the world. So God continues to act through human creative fertility; the "Temple of His body" is still being built; childbearing is participation in the Mystery of Christ.

However, as we have seen above, begetting children—though a blessed element in married life—is not the only goal of Christian marriage. This is why the second prayer insists primarily on requesting God's blessing on the couple as such. The prayer is written in form of a litany: "Bless them . . . Preserve them . . . Remember them," inviting the whole congregation to join the priest in the successive petitions. Together with Old Testament couples, the names of God-protected individuals—Noah, Jonah, the three Holy Children in Babylon, Enoch, Shem, Elijah—are also invoked because the theme of the prayer shifts from procreation to the personal devotion which merits God's help. Finally, the prayer mentions Christian saints as well: St. Helen, "who found the precious Cross," and the Forty Martyrs of Sebasteia, to whom, according to tradition, God sent crowns from Heaven. The selection of these saints points to *the Cross* as the way to kingship, as the center of the mystery of salvation and, therefore, also as the center of the mystery of marriage. This introduces the congregation directly to the crowning itself, which is the next action of the service.

2. It has been said sometimes that the use of *crowns* during the wedding service is primarily a survival of pagan rituals, as a simple expression of joy. In fact, the context and symbolism of the wedding crowns is purely Biblical. Tertullian, a second-century Christian writer and theologian, explicitly rejects the pagan use of crowns. However, when the wedding service was gradually developed, the Church used crowning to express ideas contained directly in Scripture.

The crown, traditional sign of victory in athletic competitions, is in the New Testament a sign of *victory of life over death*: "Run, then," writes St. Paul, "in such a way as to win the prize. Every athlete in training submits to strict discipline; he does so in order to be crowned with a crown that will not last; but we do it for one that will last for ever" (I Cor. 9:24-25). It is in this sense that St. John

Chrysostom sees in the wedding crowns a "symbol of victory" over unregulated sexuality (*Homily 9 on I Tim.*), which brings about corruption and death. The crown in the New Testament is also the divine and eternal reward for righteousness: "I have fought a good fight, I have finished my course, I have kept the faith; hencefore, there is laid up for me a crown of righteousness..." (II Tim. 4:7-8). "When the chief shepherd shall appear, ye shall receive a crown of glory that fadeth not away" (I Peter 5:4).

Clearly, the crown of victory and immortality belongs, first of all, to the Lord Jesus Christ Himself, crucified and risen. This is why the Church uses as the prokeimenon for the wedding service verses from Psalm 20 (21):

> Thou hast set upon their heads crowns of precious stones; they asked life of Thee and Thou gavest it them (verses 3-4).

This psalm is a solemn glorification of king and queen (in the Hebrew, the text is singular and the crown is of gold; this is found in most English versions of the psalm), and the text was always read by Christians in reference to the glory of Jesus, the Messianic King, and the Church, His bride. It is also used in the liturgy of the feast of the Ascension of Christ, with another verse chanted as prokeimenon ("Be exalted, O Lord, in Thy strength! We will sing and praise Thy power," verse 13).

The same idea appears in the solemn blessing given by the priest to the bridegroom and bride: "O Lord our God, crown them with glory and honor." The words used here are also a Scriptural quotation from Psalm 8: "Thou hast made him little less than God, and dost crown him with glory and honor" (verse 5). The entire Psalm 8 is a hymn to the dignity of man, king of creation. Jesus Himself quoted from it when He formally assumed the dignity of the Messianic King and entered Jerusalem greeted by the people: "Have you never read, 'Out of the mouth of babes and sucklings Thou hast brought perfect praise'?" (Matt. 21:16, quoting Psalm 8:2).

Christ's victory over death is best *witnessed* by those

whom we call "martyrs" (*martyros* is a Greek word for "witness"): over them, death has no power, and they already have received their crowns: "Be faithful unto death," one reads in Revelation, "and I will give you the crown of life" (2:10). In ancient Christian art, such as the mosaics of Rome and Ravenna, martyrs are always represented with crowns bestowed upon them by Christ, as signs of victory over death. This is why the prayers of the wedding service frequently mention martyrs—the Forty Martyrs of Sebasteia and the Holy Martyr Procopius—and why, during the procession, the choir sings: "O Holy Martyrs, who fought the good fight and have received your crowns: Entreat ye the Lord that He will have mercy on our souls."

These mentions of the martyrs and the identification of the crowns as symbols of martyrdom do not imply, of course, any morbid invocation of "suffering" as a constituent element of Christian marriage. The bridegroom and the bride are promised happiness and prosperity, not suffering. But, through the crowns that are placed on their heads, they are reminded of the *condition,* the central frame of reference which is making marriage a Christian marriage. This condition is the acceptance of the Gospel of Christ, the bearing of His cross in order to participate in His victory, the entry into His Kingdom in order to share in eternal life. Thus, as we have seen above, the mutual human love of a man and a woman is projected into the age to come, is crowned together with martyrs and saints by Christ Himself, becomes an eternal bond in the Mystery of Christ and the Church.

3. *The Scripture readings* include the two most revealing sections of the New Testament relative to marriage: Ephesians 5:20-33, on marriage in relation to the Mystery of Christ and the Church, and John 2:1-12, on the presence of Jesus at the marriage in Cana of Galilee.

The important point in the text of St. Paul is that the union of Christ with the Church, His body, is seen as the model—the absolute model—of the relationship between husband and wife, and even of the story of man's and woman's creation. It is not marriage which serves as a model for the understanding of Christ-Church relationships, but on the contrary this relationship is declared as a part of Christian experience which marriage is called to reflect. As we have seen above, marriage, as a sacrament, is the introduction and the transposition of man-woman relationships into the already given Kingdom of God, where Christ and the Church are one body.

The story of the marriage in Cana in Galilee has been often invoked in the past against puritanical, pseudo-monastic sectarian trends which considered marriage as impure and recommended celibacy as the only acceptable Christian ideal. This use of the passage is certainly fully legitimate: if Jesus Himself and His Mother accepted the invitation to a wedding feast, marriage is certainly blameless. Our crowning service ends with the priest giving the dismissal in the following solemn form: "May He who by His presence in Cana of Galilee declared marriage to be honorable, Christ our True God . . . have mercy on us and save us . . ."

But the text also has a more positive significance. As many historical episodes related in the Gospel of St. John, it has a double meaning. While telling of a real fact of Christ's life, it also points to a spiritual, sacramental dimension, relevant to man's salvation. We discover a double meaning of this kind in such episodes as the conversation of Christ with the Samaritan woman about "living water" (John 4; an allusion to baptism) or the discourse on the "bread of life" (John 6; an allusion to the Eucharist). So also the change of water into wine in Cana points to a transfiguration of the old into the new, a passage from death to life. As the rest of the crowning service, it announces the possibility of transforming the natural order of things into a joyful celebration of God's presence among men.

4.   Together with the Scripture readings, the sequence of the service that includes the "litany of fervent supplication," the Lord's Prayer and the partaking of a common cup reminds us vividly of the fact that the wedding service was conceived as a Eucharistic liturgy. In the present Greek usage, this Eucharistic context is emphasized even more by the singing of the *koinonikon* (communion hymn) while the bridegroom and bride partake of the cup: "I will receive the cup

of salvation and call on the name of the Lord" (Ps. 115:13).
We have seen above that the wedding service normally implied the partaking of Holy Communion by the bridal pair;
and the present Greek practice is another remnant of this
Eucharistic context of marriage.

The common cup, however, which today has unfortunately
been accepted as a substitute for communion, possesses its
own history both in liturgical tradition and custom, as sig-
nifying community of life, destiny, and responsibility.

5. After the common cup, the priest joins the hands of
the bridegroom and bride and leads them three times in a
circular procession around the lectern. Clearly, as in the case
of the rings, the circle is a symbol of eternity and emphasizes
marriage as a permanent commitment.

The meaning of this procession is also expressed in the
three troparia sung by the choir:

> Rejoice, O Isaiah! A Virgin is with child and shall bear
> a Son, Emmanuel. He is both God and man: and "Orient"
> is His name.[14] Magnifying Him, we call the Virgin blessed.

> O Holy Martyrs, who fought the good fight and have
> received your crowns: entreat ye the Lord that He will have
> mercy on our souls.

> Glory to Thee, O Christ God, the apostles' boast, the
> martyrs' joy, whose preaching was the consubstantial Trinity.

The *troparia* summarize the entire Biblical content of
Christian marriage, which is called to be a "witness"
(*martyria*) to the coming of the Kingdom of God, inaugu-
rated by the birth of the Son of God from a Virgin. The
jubilation contained in the troparia is poorly expressed in
most translations of the hymns. Thus the first words,
"Rejoice (χόρευε), O Isaiah," would be rendered more
correctly if one said "Dance in a circle, O Isaiah." The hymn
begins in fact by a call to execute a ritual *khorodia*, well

[14]"Orient" is a name of the Messiah in the Greek (LXX) version of the
Bible (see particularly Jer. 23:5) and is frequently used in Orthodox
liturgical hymnography, especially on Christmas Day when Christ is called
the "Orient from on high."

known both to the Jews of the Old Testament (David danced before the Ark of the Covenant, II Sam. 6:14) and to the ancient Greeks; and the triple circular procession of the bridal pair led by the priest around the lectern can be seen as a proper and respectful form of "liturgical dancing."

In the earlier times, the bridegroom and bride used to wear the crowns for a period of eight days following the wedding. Today, however, crowns are removed at the end of the service with appropriate short exhortations and prayers: "Receive their crowns into Thy Kingdom," says the priest, "preserving them spotless, blameless and without reproach unto ages of ages." Here lies the ultimate and true meaning of marriage as *sacrament*: whatever the difficulties, tragedies and divisiveness of human life on earth, crowns placed on the heads of two human beings are preserved in the Kingdom of God. It is up to them to decide whether this assumption of their common life by Christ will be really a decisive factor in their mutual relations and in their overall personal and social life, or whether they will prefer to live only for themselves, determined by the unredeemed, corrupt, and temporal elements which control the fallen world.

VIII.   A LITURGICAL SUGGESTION

A last question which can legitimately be asked is whether the original connection between Eucharist and marriage should not be restored in the practice of the Church. It is our opinion that it should, in a responsible and competent way, under the appropriate direction of ecclesiastical authorities.

Actually, both the Greek *Euchologion* and the Slavonic *Trebnik* require that the service be held "after the Divine Liturgy," while the priest is still "standing in the Sanctuary." Since this requirement is never fulfilled in practice, so that the connection between Eucharist and marriage does not appear at all in the way crowning is celebrated (generally in the afternoon), a restoration of the original way of celebrating crowning in the framework of the liturgy itself (see above, Chapter IV) would be the best way—pastorally and liturgically—to manifest the true dimensions of Christian marriage.

Clearly, the betrothal service is to be celebrated separately on a previous day, possibly on the eve of the wedding itself. The crowning would then take place during the regular Sunday liturgy according to the following:

- the usual exclamation: "Blessed is the Kingdom."

- the Great Litany with the additional petitions from the crowning service.

- the three wedding prayers, each followed by one of the antiphons of the liturgy (however, the antiphons may also be omitted, after the pattern of the liturgy celebrated in conjunction with Vespers on the eve of great feasts).

- the crowning.

- the Little Entrance, the Trisagion and the Scripture readings followed by the rest of the Divine Liturgy.

- after taking Holy Communion, the bridegroom and bride would also partake in the Common Cup, blessed with the appropriate prayers.

- the triple circular procession ("Rejoice, O Isaiah").

- the removal of crowns and the end of the service.

This order would not prolong the liturgy for more than ten minutes and would give to the crowning service its true and original place in the liturgical action of the whole Church. This service would, of course, not be performed in cases of "mixed marriages" or "remarriages." In those cases, the joint partaking of Holy Communion being excluded, the service would be celebrated separately from the Divine Liturgy.

IX. SUCCESSIVE MARRIAGES

We have mentioned several times already that the Church very consistently in its entire canonical and liturgical tradition maintains that second marriage is inconsistent with the Christian norm and is tolerated only by condescension to human weakness (I Corinthians 7:9). It also may be recognized as a second chance, given to a man or a woman, to enter into a real marriage in Christ when a first union was a mistake (for even Church blessing cannot always magically repair a human mistake!). The case of saints—for example St. Tamara, Queen of Georgia—who entered a second marriage, indicates that the norm, according to which only the first marriage is "real," should not be understood in a juridical, legalistic way.

It remains, however, that St. Basil the Great (d. 379), in his canon 4, defines that those who enter a second marriage after either widowhood or divorce must undergo penance, i.e., abstain from communion for one or two years. A third marriage implies a penance of three, four, or even five years. "Such a marriage," writes St. Basil, "we do not consider as marriage, but polygamy, or rather adultery, which requires a definite penance" (*ibid.*).

Clearly, since marriage—in the time of St. Basil—was performed through the Eucharist, exclusion from communion meant that these marriages (the second or the third) could be concluded only as civil agreements. Only after the years of penance were the couples readmitted among the "faithful," and permitted to receive communion. Their marriage was then recognized as a Christian marriage.

The norms described by St. Basil were enforced until at least the ninth century. St. Theodore Studite (759-826) and the canons attributed to St. Nicephorus, Patriarch of Constantinople (806-815), are witnesses of this. "Those who entered a second marriage are not crowned and are not admitted to receive the most pure Mysteries for two years; those who enter a third marriage are excommunicated for five

years" (Canon of Nicephorus, 2). It is not so much the
strictness of these rules which deserves attention—in general,
excommunication was practiced much more widely in the
early Church than it is today—but the Church's concern for
maintaining the absolute uniqueness of Christian marriage.

Only when the rite of marriage was separated from the
Liturgy could the Church express more leniency in crowning
second or third marriages, while retaining its rule concerning
communion. In the *Canonical Answers* of Nicetas, Metropolitan of Herakleia (thirteenth century), we read: "Strictly
speaking, one should not crown those who marry a second
time, but the custom of the Great Church (i.e., the Church
of Constantinople) does not maintain this strictness: it
tolerates that marriage crowns be placed on the heads of
those couples . . . They must, however, abstain from communion to the Holy Mysteries for one or two years."[15]

In our own contemporary service book, the "order of
second marriage" is strikingly different from the normal rite.
It is nothing more than a short expansion of the betrothal
service. It does not start with the exclamation, "Blessed is
the Kingdom . . ." (which connects marriage with the
Eucharist), but with the usual "Blessed is our God . . ."
followed by the reading of the beginning prayers: "O
Heavenly King . . ." etc. The Great Litany is reduced to a
few simple petitions and only the two last short prayers of
the betrothal service are read. The long "prayer of the rings"
is replaced with a penitential supplication asking for "forgiveness of transgressions," for "purification" and "pardon." The
Biblical personalities mentioned are not the glorious couples
of the Old Testament, but Rahab the harlot (Joshua 2:1-24;
Heb. 11:31 and James 2:25), the contrite publican (Luke
18:10-14), and the good thief (Luke 23:40-43): all three
received God's forgiveness through faith and repentance. A
second prayer speaks of the bridegroom and the bride as
having been "unable to bear the heat and burden of the day
and the hot desires of the flesh" and thus having decided
to accept "the bond of a second marriage." Without any
procession towards the center of the church and without any

[15]Rallis and Potlis, *Syntagma of the Holy Canons*, V, p. 441.

new beginning, the Crowning is then performed starting with the third and shortest prayer of the normal order.

This order for "a second marriage" is so strikingly different, so deliberately penitential that, in some cases when a second marriage is obviously a happy event, it is difficult to justify its use and to give an acceptable explanation of it to the couple and to the congregation. Orthodox rubrics recommend that it be used only if both the bridegroom and bride are entering a second marriage. This reservation is difficult to explain theologically because, as we have seen above, the scriptural and canonical tradition of the Church would certainly not consider as fully "normal" a marriage when even one party was already married before.

It is our opinion that some discretion in the use of the prayers should, therefore, be left to the priest celebrating each given marriage. He could, for example, consider it proper to use the structure of the "second marriage" rite, but replace those prayers which he considers as obviously inappropriate to the given couple by prayers taken from the normal service of Crowning. In no case, however, should he ignore the norms of Christian marriage, which ideally can be only unique, and the necessary difference between the first marriage and all forms of "remarriage."

A second chance (or a condescension for human earthly desires), second marriage is admitted only as long as the ideal norm of an eternal union in the name of Christ and according to the laws of the future divine Kingdom is maintained. The fact that the Church eventually included crowning in the service for second marriages indicates that they too can realize this ideal, whatever the formal irregularities. It is this positive ideal which was proclaimed consistently by the canons and the liturgy, rather than an abstract and legal notion of indissolubility. Practically, this pastoral "economy" ("housekeeping" of the Church) goes even as far as to allow a third marriage, but formally forbids a fourth. In the canons of St. Basil and St. Nicephorus, quoted above, fourth marriage is not mentioned at all even as a possibility. The famous case of Emperor Leo VI, the Wise (886-912), which provoked long discussions and even a schism, ended with the publication of a *Tome of Union* (920) which prohibited fourth marriage while permitting a third only until the age of forty.[16]

Obviously, there cannot be any theological reason why the number of possible successive marriages for a Christian is limited to three: the limit is only disciplinary and it is defined by "economy," which is not—as it is too often thought—an open door to limitless compromise. There is indeed a positive Christian discipline. The earthly needs of the "old man" can be met, and even respected, as a lesser evil; but man's salvation itself requires that he be taught to overcome anything which does not belong to the Kingdom of God, already present in the Church.

X. CONDITIONS FOR MARRIAGE

Christian marriage is essentially a meeting of two beings in love, a human love which can be transformed, by the sacramental grace of the Holy Spirit, into an eternal bond, indissoluble even by death. But this sacramental transformation does not suppress the *human* character of the whole complex of emotions, actions, joys, or vicissitudes connected with marriage: acquaintance, dating, courtship, the decision itself and, finally, common life with its difficult responsibilities. The New Testament teaching on marriage is addressed to concrete human beings, who are not only committed to Christ, but are also living in the conditions of the present world. The various rules and disciplines which have been and still are proposed to Christians in connection with marriage are there to protect and preserve the fundamental meaning of marriage in the concrete conditions of human life. These rules are not ends in themselves, for they would be substitutes for love; but their aim is to protect both

[16]Rallis and Potlis, op. cit., V. p. 4-10. English translation below, Appendix III, pp. 106-07.

the divine and the human reality of marriage from the consequences of man's fall.

Freedom of choice and decision is the first condition of true Christian marriage, which Orthodox canonical tradition tries to maintain. There are several canons against forceful abduction of women, which also nullify marriages concluded against their will (St. Basil, canons 22 and 30). The guilty man is excommunicated (Chalcedon, canon 27), as well as the consenting woman (St. Basil, canon 38). There are also texts which require a sufficiently long period to elapse between betrothal and marriage; legally assimilated with marriage and protected as such, this period obviously served as a test for the decision itself (cf. Sixth Ecumenical Council, or "Quinisext," canon 98).

If the protection of free choice in the marriage decision is obviously justified, other stipulations of the ancient canons and of the Christian emperors seem to be determined only by social, legal or psychological presuppositions of the past. When, for example, the Code of Emperor Justinian, condoned by the Church, admits the ages of 14 and 12, for men and women respectively, as the lowest age limit for marriage, one must admit that modern society is closer to the Christian ideal of man when it advances the limit a little closer to adulthood! Very liberal on this point, the Byzantine legal and canonical tradition appears to be unduly restrictive when it sees obstacles to marriage in relatively distant degrees of family affinity or relationship.

In Judaism, marriages between close relatives, even first cousins, were accepted and often encouraged; Roman law forbade marriage in different generations (for example, an uncle with his niece), but permitted union between first cousins. Christianity alone began to limit very strictly marriages not only between close blood-relatives, but also between "in-laws." Thus, following several decrees of emperors Theodosius and Justinian, the Sixth Ecumenical Council ("Quinisext") decreed that "he who shall marry with the daughter of his father;"[17] or a father or son with a mother and daughter; or a father and son with two girls who are

---

[17] A half-sister.

sisters; or a mother and daughter with two brothers; or two brothers with two sisters, fall under the canon of seven years (of excommunication), provided they openly separate from this unlawful union" (canon 54).

This extraordinary text can be explained perhaps by a general Christian concern for preserving human relations as they were once created, by birth or marriage, to prevent family misunderstandings and tensions, which could be created by courtships and "falling in love." This concern may have been justified when large families, including several generations of relatives, used to live together. On the other hand, the abstract principle—always strictly maintained in Roman law—concerning the degrees of relationships must have influenced the council. According to that principle, a married couple is legally considered as one single person; and thus, for example, a man was considered in the *first degree* of parenthood with his sister-in-law. If his wife died, he was therefore not allowed to remarry her sister simply in virtue of the principle that marriages, in Byzantine law, were forbidden up to the *seventh degree* of relationship.

Obviously, today it does not seem either necessary or desirable to apply strictly those canons which are based on social and legal principles of the past, and which do not correspond to any permanent theological or spiritual value. The only pastoral consideration which the Church must maintain is the genetic risk contained in consanguineous marriages.

Even more surprising are the stipulations of Justinian's Code (V, 4), followed again by the Sixth Council, which legally identify "spiritual" relationships with blood affinity: "spiritual" relationship was created by sponsorship at Baptism. Thus canon 53 of Quinisext forbids not only marriages between sponsors and their God-children, but even, specifically, between the sponsor and the mother of the newly baptized child (should she become a widow). Perhaps the canons aim at protecting the particular responsibility of the God-parents, whose interest should be concentrated exclusively upon the Christian upbringing of their God-children, and which should not be distracted by marital plans.

The desire to conform with the ancient legal norms should not obscure, in our own eyes, the real and tremendous responsibility of priests, of educators, of parents, and, first, of all, of the young couples themselves, in connection with marriage. It is certainly not by simply fulfilling legal and canonical norms that one can conclude a truly Christian marriage. Christian marriage is essentially a *positive commitment* of the couple, not only to each other, but first to Christ, a commitment realized in and through the Eucharist. If this commitment does not occur, the fulfillment of all the legal stipulations concerning Christian marriage will have no meaning at all.

But what if such a commitment is not possible, and not even desired, by the couple? What if marriage is considered as only a social event, or a legal arrangement on property rights, or simply a way of legitimizing sex?

These are the problems which the priest must solve so often when he is being approached by couples whose relation to the Church is only peripheral. His responsibility then is to make them understand the meaning of Christian marriage; and he should consider seriously, each time, whether it is not preferable to postpone marriage plans, or even to marry at a civil ceremony, rather than engage in a Church marriage without understanding, or without accepting its true meaning.

This question arises, in particular, in connection with "mixed" marriages.

XI. "MIXED" MARRIAGES

Unity of faith, i.e., a joint commitment to the Orthodox Church, is formally a condition of Church marriage. The councils of Laodicea (canons 10 and 31), of Carthage (canon 21), as well as the Fourth and the Sixth Ecumenical Councils (Chalcedon 14, Quinisext 72) forbid marriages between an Orthodox and a non-Orthodox, and stipulate that such marriages, if concluded before civil magistrates, must be dissolved.

But, of course, the problem here is not only formal. It concerns the very essence of what makes a marriage really *Christian*. It is certainly possible, without being members of the same Church, to enjoy friendship, to share interests, to experience a true character compatibility, and, of course, to "be in love" with each other. But the question is whether all these human affinities can be transformed and transfigured in the reality of the Kingdom of God if one does not share the same experience of what this Kingdom is, if one is not committed to the same and unique Faith. Is it possible to become "one body" in Christ, without participating together in His eucharistic Body and Blood? Can a couple share in the Mystery of marriage—a Mystery "which concerns Christ and the Church"—without taking part together in the Mystery of the Divine Liturgy?

These are certainly not "formal" questions, but indeed basic ones, which should confront all those who envisage contracting a "mixed" marriage. Easy solutions can, of course, be found in confessional relativism—"there is not much difference between our churches"—or in simply eliminating the Eucharist from the center of Christian life. The latter way is, unfortunately, suggested by our present practice of using the same order of crowning for both a wedding between two Orthodox Christians and in a "mixed" marriage. The very possibility of this practice comes, as we have shown above, from the gradual desacralization of marriage, which ended in its separation from the Eucharist. In the early Church the meaning of the canons forbidding mixed marriages was understood by all; for everyone knew that an Orthodox and a non-Orthodox could not participate together in the Eucharist, where marriages were normally blessed. The recent Protestant practice of encouraging "intercommunion" between separated Christians, and the even more recent Roman Catholic partial endorsement of this practice, have confused the issue even more. The personal and total commitment to the visible Church of Christ in the Eucharist may, in fact, be replaced through these practices by a vague and relativistic religiosity in which these sacraments play a very subsidiary role.[18]

By refusing the practice of "intercommunion," the Orthodox Church does not refuse Christian unity. It defends, on the contrary, the true and full unity and rejects all possible substitutes for it. Similarly, in marriage, the Church desires that the couple be fully united in Christ; and therefore considers that only those marriages are fully sacramental and truly Christian, which join two beings in a full unity of faith and which, as such, are sealed by the Eucharist.

"Mixed" marriages have often happened in the past in spite of the canonical prohibitions listed above. In our own pluralistic society, where the Orthodox represent only a small minority, they represent a very large and ever-increasing percentage of all marriages blessed in our churches, and also, unfortunately, outside of Orthodoxy. We all know that some of them lead to the creation of happy families, and it would be unwise and utopian to discourage them all. Actually, it may well be that some of such marriages end up being more durable and happier than those contracted by nominal Orthodox who never heard about the meaning of Christian marriage and who never accepted personally and responsibly any true Christian commitment.

All this being unquestionably true, it remains that the Gospel calls us not to partial truth, and not even to human "happiness" only. The Lord says: "You must be perfect, as your heavenly Father is perfect" (Matthew 5:48). There is no Christianity without *striving* for perfection. Religious indifference, or acceptance of the Christian faith as only a peripheral area of existence, excludes the yearning for perfection to which Christ calls us. The Church can never reconcile itself with such indifference and relativism.

It should be clear, for example, that an Orthodox priest can never bless a marriage between an Orthodox and a non-Christian. It would be obviously improper to invoke the name of Jesus Christ in the marriage service for a person who does not recognize Him as his or her Lord. Such an invocation

[18]On the Orthodox (very negative) view on "intercommunion" between separated Christians, see *St. Vladimir's Theological Quarterly*, vol. 27, 1983, No. 4.

would actually be disrespectful, not only towards the Lord, but also towards this person and towards his or her convictions (or lack of convictions). When the non-Orthodox partner of a prospective marriage is a baptized Christian, the blessing given in the Orthodox Church implies the conviction of St. Paul that "the unbelieving husband is consecrated through his wife, and the unbelieving wife is consecrated through her husband" (I Cor. 7:14), although most probably, this text speaks of those marriages where one partner has been converted since marriage rather than where a member of the Church marries a non-member. In any case, the Church, in each of such cases, hopes that religious unity of the family will eventually be restored and that one day both partners will be united in Orthodoxy.

The regulation adopted by some Orthodox dioceses (and until lately by the Roman Catholic Church) to require the partners of a mixed marriage to sign a pledge, promising to baptize and raise their children in Orthodoxy, appears—at least to this writer—rather questionable, both in its principle and its effects. The legal formality of this procedure is not in tune with the very idea of Christian freedom and responsibility. Either the Orthodox partner is strong enough in his or her convictions to give a proper religious direction to the children (and hopefully bring the whole family into the Church), or he will give up anyway. A firm pastoral attitude should, however, be adopted towards those who marry outside of the Orthodox Church. To have one's marriage blessed outside of the Church is obviously a betrayal of the sacramental grace received from it at baptism and is, in fact, inconsistent with Church membership.

Many of the problems related to mixed marriages would be clarified in the eyes of all—Orthodox and non-Orthodox alike—if the ancient practice of integrating the marriage ceremony into the Eucharistic liturgy were revived. This would imply that a different, extra-eucharistic ceremony would be used for mixed marriages (as well as for second or third marriages between Orthodox). The very impossibility to bless mixed marriages during the liturgy would be eloquent enough to show, firstly, the nature of full sacramental marriage in

Church; secondly, the pastoral tolerance exercised by the Church when it has to bless mixed marriage; and, thirdly, the clear desire of the Church to have, one day, the mixed marriage fulfilled in unity of faith and in joint participation in the Eucharist.

XII. DIVORCE

The Roman Catholic insistence on the legal "indissolubility" of marriage and the total impossibility for divorcees to remarry, while their former partner is still alive, has long been and still is the subject of much debate. Much too often the Orthodox position on this issue is defined simply by contrast to Roman Catholicism. Is it right to say simply that "the Orthodox Church admits divorce"?

The Roman Catholic traditional view and canonical regulations on divorce and remarriage are based on two presuppositions: 1) that marriage is a legal contract, and that for Christians this contract is legally indissoluble; 2) that the marriage contract concerns only earthly life, and that, therefore, it is legally dissolved by the death of one of the partners. The Orthodox approach starts, as we have seen earlier, from different presuppositions:

1) That marriage is a sacrament conferred upon the partners in the Body of the Church through the priest's blessing; that, as any sacrament, it pertains to the eternal life in the Kingdom of God; and that it is, therefore, not dissolved by the death of one of the partners, but creates between them—if they so wish and if "it is given to them" (Matthew 19:11)—an eternal bond.

2) That, as sacrament, marriage is not a magical act, but a gift of grace. The partners, being humans, may have made a mistake in soliciting the grace of marriage when they were not ready for it; or they may prove to be unable to make this grace fructify. In those cases, the Church may admit the fact that the grace was not "received," tolerate separation and

allow remarriage. But, of course, she never encourages any remarriage—we have seen that even in the case of widowers—because of the eternal character of the marriage bond; but only tolerates it when, in concrete cases, it appears as the best solution for a given individual.

The repeated condemnation of divorce by Christ Himself is well known: "For your hardness of heart Moses allowed you to divorce your wives, but from the beginning it was not so. And I say to you: whoever divorces his wife except for unchastity, and marries another, commits adultery; and he who marries a divorced woman, commits adultery" (Matthew 19:8-9; cf. 5:31-32; Mark 10:2-9; Luke 16:18).[19] However, the possibility of divorce on grounds of "unchastity," and the even more general admission by St. Paul that a wife can separate herself from her husband (II Cor. 7:11), clearly show that the New Testament does not understand indissolubility of marriage as total suppression of human freedom. And freedom implies the possibility of sin, as well as its consequences; ultimately, sin can destroy marriage.

However, nowhere does the New Testament explicitly condone remarriage after divorce. St. Paul, who discourages but permits the remarriage of widowers, is very negative concerning the remarriage of divorcees: "To the married I give charge, not I but the Lord, that the wife should not separate from her husband—but if she does, let her remain single or else be reconciled to her husband—and that the husband should not divorce his wife" (I Cor. 6: 10-11).

How did the Church respond to this New Testament attitude? The Fathers, in their great majority, followed St. Paul in discouraging any form of remarriage, either after widowhood or after divorce. Athenagoras, an Athenian philosopher and convert who wrote an *Apology of the Christians* around the year 177, is the spokesman of all the ancient Fathers of the Church when he, after specifically calling a remarried divorcee "adulteress," adds also that "He who rids

[19]Note that the exception concerning divorce on grounds of "unchastity" (πορνεία) is found only in the Gospel of Matthew. The prohibition of divorce is unreserved in Christ's words, as reported by St. Mark and St. Luke.

himself of his first wife, although she is dead, is an adulterer in a certain disguised manner" (PG 6, col. 968).

But, at the same time, the Church never considered the Gospel as a system of legal prescriptions which human society could adopt overnight. The Gospel was to be accepted as a commitment, as a pledge of the Kingdom to come; it presupposed constant personal struggle against sin and evil, but it never could be reduced to a system of *legal* "obligations" or "duties."

Thus, the Christian empire continued to admit divorce and remarriage as a regular social institution. The laws of the Christian emperors, especially Constantine, Theodosius and Justinian, defined the various legal grounds and conditions on which divorce and remarriage were permissible. It is impossible for us here to enumerate them all. It will be sufficient to say that they were relatively lenient. Divorce by simple mutual consent was tolerated until a law issued by emperor Theodosius II in 449, which forbade it; but it was again authorized by Justin II in 566. The law of Justin II was repealed only in the eighth century. Throughout all that period, divorce, with right of remarriage, was granted not only on the grounds of adultery, but also on such grounds as political treason, planning of murder, disappearance for five years or more, unjustified accusation of adultery and, finally, monastic vows of one of the partners.[20]

No Father of the Church ever denounced these imperial laws as contrary to Christianity. There was an evident consensus of opinion that considered them as inevitable. Emperors like Justinian I sincerely tried to issue legislation inspired by Christianity and, when formulating it, used competent advice of bishops and theologians. Among the latter, many opposed imperial will when it infringed upon Christian orthodoxy; but none opposed their legislation on divorce. Many, on the contrary, mentioned this legislation as a fact: "He who cannot keep continence after the death of his first wife," writes St. Epiphanius of Cyprus (d. 403), "or who has separated from his wife for a valid motive, as fornication, adultery, or another misdeed, if he takes another wife, or if the

---

[20]See especially the Novella 22 of Justinian.

wife takes another husband, the divine word does not condemn him nor exclude him from the Church or the life; but she tolerates it rather on account of his weakness" (*Against heresies,* 69, PG 41, col. 1024 C–1025A).

Pastoral exhortations on the evil of divorce are of course innumerable; but the toleration of existing state laws, as well as of the "facts of life," as they occurred, is equally evident on the part of all, in both East and West.

Was this simple lenience or a capitulation? Certainly not. During this entire period, without a single known exception, the Church remained faithful to the *norm* set by the New Testament revelation: *only the first and unique marriage was blessed in Church during the Eucharist.*

We have seen above that second and third marriages, after widowhood, were concluded at a civil ceremony only, and implied a penance of one to five years of excommunication. After this period of penance, the couple was again considered as fully members of the Church. A more prolonged penance was required for married divorcees, i.e., *seven years*: "He who leaves the wife given him, and shall take another is guilty of adultery by the sentence of the Lord. And it has been decreed by our Fathers that they who are such must be 'weepers' for a year, 'hearers' for two years, 'prostrators' for three years, and in the seventh year to stand with the faithful and thus be counted worthy of the Oblation" (Sixth Ecumenical Council, canon 87).

There were, of course, innumerable stipulations concerning the difference between the guilty and the innocent partners in a divorce; and, in practice, the pastoral "economy" of the Church certainly has shown occasionally more leniency than this text implies. Nevertheless, the classification of the marrying divorcees among the adulterers—in strict conformity with the Gospel text—implied that they spent sufficient time standing in Church not among the faithful, but at the doorway, with the "weepers," the "hearers" (i.e., those who listened to Scripture, but were not admitted to the sacraments), and the "prostrators" (i.e., those who held, during certain parts of the services, a prostrated position, instead of sitting or standing).

The Church, therefore, neither "recognized" divorce, nor "gave" it. Divorce was considered as a grave sin; but the Church never failed in giving to sinners a "new chance," and was ready to readmit them if they repented.

Only after the tenth century, when it received from the emperors the legal monopoly of registering and validating all marriages (see above, Chapter V), was the Church obliged to "issue divorces." It did it generally in conformity with civil legislation of the Roman Empire, and later with that of the various countries in which it developed. But this new situation greatly obliterated in the consciousness of the faithful the uniqueness of the Christian doctrine on marriage. Both the Church marriage and the "Church divorce" appeared as mere formality giving external legality to acts which were generally quite illegitimate from the Christian point of view.

Practically, and in full conformity with Scripture and Church tradition, I would suggest that our Church authorities stop "giving divorces" (since the latter anyway are secured through civil courts), and rather, on the basis of a recognition, based upon the civil divorce, that marriage does not in fact exist, issue "permissions to remarry." Of course, in each particular case pastoral counseling and investigation should make sure that reconciliation is impossible; and the "permission to remarry" should entail at least some forms of penance (in conformity with each individual case) and give the right to a Church blessing according to the rite of "second marriage."

Such a move will make the position of our Church clear and will give the priests an opportunity to exercise more fruitfully their ministry of explanation, guidance and psychological healing.

XIII. FAMILY AND FAMILY PLANNING

Jesus Himself, on the eve of His death, at the solemn moment when He participated with His disciples in their last Supper together, recalled the joy of childbirth: "When a woman is delivered of the child, she no longer remembers

the anguish, for joy that a child is born into the world"
(John 16:21). And all parents know that the "anguish"
which is so totally forgotten when the child comes is not
only the physical pain of the mother, but also all the human
anxieties, the financial worries, which all men and women
feel so often before they have children. All this is totally
gone when a new little creature, helpless and totally "your
own," appears in the family and desperately needs love and
concern.

And then there is Jesus' attitude towards children:
"Calling to him a child, he put him in the midst of them
and said, 'Truly I say to you, unless you turn and become
like children, you will never enter the Kingdom of heaven' "
(Matthew 18:2). Can one understand the full meaning of this
warning by the Lord—probably one of the most revealing of
the entire Gospel—if one deliberately deprives oneself from
having children?

In fact, childbirth and raising of children are indeed a
great joy and God's blessing. There can be no Christian
marriage without an immediate and impatient desire of both
parents to receive and share in this joy. A marriage where
children are unwelcome is founded upon a defective, egoistic
and fleshly form of love. In giving life to others, man
imitates God's creative act and, if he refuses to do so, he
not only rejects his Creator, but also distorts his own humanity; for there is no humanity without an "image and
likeness of God," i.e., without a conscious, or unconscious
desire to be a true imitator of the life-creating Father of all.

However, we have seen above (Chapter I) that one of
the essential differences between the Old Testament Judaic
conception of marriage and the Christian one was that, for
the ancient Jews, marriage was a means for procreation only,
while, for Christians, it is an end in itself—a union of two
beings, in love, reflecting the union between Christ and the
Church. And, indeed, neither in the Gospels nor in St. Paul
does one find the idea that childbirth "justifies" marriage.
Neither does one find that idea in patristic literature. In his
magnificent Homily 20 on the Epistle to the Ephesians, St.
John Chrysostom defines marriage as a "union" and a

"mystery," and only occasionally mentions childbirth (see
A Select Library of the Nicene and Post Nicene Fathers, vol.
XIII, Grand Rapids, Mich., 1956, pp. 143-152; see below,
Appendix II).

Modern Western Christian thinking and practice are ut-
terly confused on this point; and the mass media, commenting
upon and often distorting and misinterpreting the papal en-
cyclicals that forbid artificial birth control to Roman Catholics,
contribute very little to a possible clarification.

The point is that, until quite recently, Western thought
on sex and marriage was entirely and almost exclusively
dominated by the teaching of St. Augustine (d. 430). The
peculiarity of St. Augustine's point of view was that he
considered sex and sexual instinct as the channel through
which the guilt for the "original sin" of Adam was trans-
mitted to Adam's posterity. Marriage, therefore, was itself
sinful in as much as it presupposed sex, and could be justified only "through childbirth." Consequently, if childbirth
is artificially prevented, sexual intercouse—even in lawful
marriage—is fundamentally sinful.

The Orthodox Church—as does the Roman Catholic—
recognizes the sanctity of St. Augustine, but his doctrinal
authority in Orthodoxy is far from being as absolute as it
used to be in the West. And even if, in Eastern Christian
monastic literature, sex is sometimes practically identified
with sin, the general Tradition of the Church holds very
firmly the decisions of the Council of Gangra (see below
Appendix III), which radically rejects the opinion which condemned marriage. And certainly, if the sexual instinct—in its
perverted and "fallen" form—is often connected with sin, it
is certainly not the only channel through which sinfulness
spreads throughout human generations. But marriage itself
is a sacrament; i.e., in man-woman relations, it is being redeemed by the Cross of Christ, transfigured by the grace of
the Spirit, and transformed by love into an eternal bond.

If sex equals sin, and if childbirth alone can relieve the
guilt, both marriage and procreation are no better than poor
substitutes for the only true Christian ideal—celibacy. They
have practically no positive Christian significance of their

own; and of course, marital intercourse which avoids child-birth is clearly sinful, if only one adopts the Augustinian view of sex and marriage. Even if the recent papal encyclical *Humanae vitae,* prohibiting artificial birth control, is not based on Augustinism, but rather stresses the positive concern for human life, it remains that ideas about the sinfulness of sex dominated Roman Catholic thought in the past and, indirectly, prevent the contemporary leadership from chang-ing its attitude towards birth-control. For how can it con-tradict that which was its standard teaching for so many years?

The Orthodox Church, for its part, has never committed itself formally and officially on the issue. This does not mean, however, that the questions of birth control and family planning are indifferent to Orthodox Christians and that their Christian commitment does not have practical implica-tions in this issue. As we have shown earlier, this Christian commitment implies the belief

— that childbirth is the natural, holy and necessary ele-ment in Christian marriage,
— that to give life is a God-like privilege of man, which he has no right to refuse if he wants to preserve the "image and likeness of God" given him at his creation.

The papal encyclical *Humanae vitae* includes remarkable statements on both of these points and, therefore, should not be dismissed simply because it is papal.

However, the issue of family planning has also other aspects, which are widely acknowledged and discussed today. For example, if the "life" given by parents to their children is to be a fully human life, it cannot involve only physical existence, but also parental care, education and decent living. When they beget children, parents must be ready to fulfill all these responsibilities. There obviously are economic, social or psychological situations where no guarantees can be given in this respect. And there is sometimes even a near certainty that the newly born children will live in hunger and psycho-logical misery.

In those situations, various forms of family planning, as old as humanity itself, have been always known to men and women. Total continence is one radical way of birth control. But is it compatible with true married life? And is not continence itself a form of limiting the God-bestowed power of giving and perpetuating life? However, both the New Testament and Church tradition consider continence as an acceptable form of family planning. Recent Roman Catholic teaching also recommends periodic continence, but forbids the "artificial" means, such as the "pill." But is there a real difference between the means called "artificial" and those considered "natural"? Is continence really "natural"? Is not any medical control of human functions "artificial"? Should it, therefore, be condemned as sinful? And finally, a serious theological question: is anything "natural" necessarily "good"? For even St. Paul saw that continence can lead to "burning." Is not science able to render childbirth more humane, by controlling it, just as it controls food, habitat and health?

Straight condemnation of birth-control fails to give satisfactory answers to all these questions. It has never been endorsed by the Orthodox Church as a whole, even if, at times, local Church authorities may have issued statements on the matter identical to that of the Pope. In any case, it has never been the Church's practice to give moral guidance by issuing standard formulas claiming universal validity on questions which actually require a personal act of conscience. There are forms of birth control which will be acceptable, and even unavoidable, for certain couples, while others will prefer avoiding them. This is particularly true of the "pill."

The question of birth control and of its acceptable forms can only be solved by individual Christian couples. They can make the right decision only if they accept their Christian commitment with ultimate seriousness, if they believe in the providence of God, if they avoid being concerned too much with material security ("Do not lay up for yourself treasures on earth," Matthew 6:19), if they realize that children are a great joy and a gift of God, if their love is not a selfish and egotistic one, if they remember that love reduced to sexual pleasure is not true love. For example, in an affluent American society, there is practically never a sufficient reason to avoid children in the first two years of marriage. In any case, the advice of a good father confessor could help much in taking the right "first step" in married life.

XIV. ABORTION

Following Scripture, Orthodox canon law formally identifies abortion with murder and requires the excommunication of all those involved: "Those who give drugs procuring abortion and those who receive poisons to kill the foetus are subjected to the penalty of murder" (Sixth Ecumenical Council, canon 91).

In his canon 2 dealing with abortion, St. Basil the Great specifically excludes any consideration which would allow abortion at an early period of pregnancy. "She who purposely destroys the foetus shall suffer the punishment of murder, and we pay no attention to the distinction as to whether the foetus was formed or unformed."

The penitential discipline of the early Church required that "murderers" be admitted to a reconciliation with the Church and to Holy Communion only at their deathbed if at that time they repented. However, exceptions were admitted. The council of Ancyra specifically allows some exceptions for those involved in abortion: "Concerning women who commit fornication and destroy that which they have conceived or who are employed in making drugs for abortion, a former decree excluded them until the hour of death and to this some have assented. Nevertheless, being desirous to use somewhat greater leniency, we have ordained that they fulfill ten years (of penance) ..." (canon 21).

In order to understand fully the position of the Orthodox Church on the issue of abortion, one can also refer to the solemn celebration by the Church of such feasts as the Conception of St. John the Baptist (Sept. 24), the Conception of the Theotokos (Dec. 8) and indeed the Feast of the Annunciation (March 25), when Christ Himself was conceived in the womb of the Virgin. The celebration of these

Feasts clearly implies that human life—and, in those cases, the life of John, of the Theotokos, and of Jesus, as Man— begins at the moment of conception and not at a later moment, when, supposedly, the foetus becomes "viable."

If one remains in the Biblical and Christian perspective, there is no way of avoiding the fact that abortion is an interruption of human life. It can in no way be justified by the arguments which are usually accepted in our permissive and secularized society: the physical or psychological discomfort of the mother, over-population, financial hardships, social insecurity, etc. These are indeed evils which need to be cured, but the cure cannot be achieved by killing innocent victims who possess a full potential for a normal human life. If abortion is accepted, as a normal procedure in facing the ills of society, there is strictly no reason why killing could not be accepted as a "solution" (Hitler's "final solution" of the Jewish problem!) in other situations, particularly in illness and old age. If the "terminally" sick (and old people are generally all "terminal") were put quietly to death, what a psychological relief for those psychologically and materially responsible for their continued existence! But what a horrible and totally unhuman perspective for society! And it is quite frightening to discover how close to its realization we already are.

For Christians, killing is always evil in whatever circumstances it occurs, killing at war not excluded. St. Basil the Great requires that soldiers who have been directly involved in killing in war do penance for three years (canon 13). However, by not condoning total pacifism (though admitting it sometimes), the Church recognized that killing at war is not fully identical to murder since it occurs (at least, in principle) *to save other lives.* Other instances, when a killing occurs *for the defense* of innocent life, this cannot be seen, strictly speaking, as murder. However, the attitude of St. Basil towards the soldiers indicates that even in these cases, killing is evil, even if possibly *a lesser evil* than a passive acceptance of violence by others. By analogy, one may consider that in the extreme (and very rare) case when the interruption of the life of the foetus is the only means of saving the life of the mother, it may also be considered a "lesser evil." However, in those cases, the horrible responsibility for the decision is to be taken with full awareness of the fact that killing remains killing.

So Orthodox Christians do possess a clear guidance of their Church in this fateful issue, as far as their own personal and family responsibilities are concerned. They will also certainly oppose legislation liberalizing abortion, since this legislation is a clear sign of dehumanization and cynicism in our society. They will remember, however, that a morally valid stand against abortion implies an especially responsible care for the millions of miserable, hungry, uneducated and unwanted children that come into the world without assurance of a decent life.

XV. MARRIED CLERGY

The New Testament includes positive information about the fact that at least some of the apostles—including St. Peter—were married men; and the married state was considered as normal for those ordained to succeed in their ministry: "A bishop must be above reproach, the husband of one wife, temperate, sensible, dignified, hospitable . . . He must manage his own household well, keeping his children submissive and respectful in every way" (I Tim. 3:2-4).

The admission of married men to the priesthood and the episcopate was, however, conditioned—in the early canons— by the fully Christian character of their marriage: "the man who has been married twice after baptism, or has had a concubine, cannot become a bishop, presbyter, or deacon, or a member of the clergy altogether" (Apostolic canon 17). We have seen above that second marriage was only tolerated for laymen. The canon just quoted excludes clergy from this toleration. For, indeed, ordination implies preaching of the full Christian Truth, and, in particular, of the Christian concept of the unique marriage according to "Christ and the

Church." The requirement actually extends to the clergyman's wife: "He who married a widow, or a divorced woman, or a harlot, or a slave, or an actress,[21] cannot be a bishop, or a presbyter, or a deacon, or enter any other order of the clergy" (Apostolic canon 18). But this again is fully consistent with the Christian ideal of absolute monogamy, which alone can be sacramentally sealed by the Eucharist and acquire a full sacramental meaning. Let us remember that second marriages were not blessed in Church.

But the requirement does not cover civil marriages contracted "before baptism," i.e., outside of the Church. As we have seen above, these are not considered as "marriages" and cannot prevent the ordination of a man who subsequently was married again in the Church.

Very early, the canons of the Church stipulated that if married men could be admitted into the clergy, clergy in major orders could not marry after their ordination (Apostolic canon 26). However, in the fourth century, the Council of Ancyra still allowed deacons to marry, if, at their ordination, they declared their intention of doing so (canon 10). This practice was formally forbidden by Emperor Justinian in his novella 123; and the Quinisext (or "Sixth ecumenical") Council, as in many other instances, confirmed imperial legislation: "Since it is declared in the apostolic canons that of those who are advanced to the clergy unmarried, only readers and cantors are able to marry; we also, maintaining this, determine that henceforth it is in nowise lawful for any subdeacon, deacon or presbyter, after his ordination, to contract matrimony, but if he shall have dared to do so, let him be deposed..." (canon 6).

This canonical legislation, forbidding marriage after ordination, is motivated by exactly the same considerations as those found in canons stressing *maturity* and *stability* as essential requirements for members of the clergy. In the early and medieval Church, the rule forbidding ordination before the age of thirty (Sixth Ecumenical, canon 14) was strictly applied. If, today, the Church is much less strict on the

[21]Slavery and "show business" implied at least the suspicion of light morals.

problem of "canonical age"—ordination of such younger men to the priesthood is a standard practice—it still maintains the requirement of maturity. And, indeed, a man desiring marriage, and seeking a wife, necessarily lacks stability, whatever his age. Dating, preferential treatment, preoccupation with externals are legitimate and unavoidable aspects of his behavior. But these cannot be considered as legitimate for a man in charge of human souls, and who is supposed to be dedicated only to bringing them into the Kingdom of God. Thus, only those men who have made a firm and final decision for their married life or celibacy are admitted to the diaconate and the priesthood.

The prohibition of marriage after ordination is, of course, of different nature than that which requires that a priest be married only once, and that his wife be neither a widow, nor a divorcee. While in the first case, what is involved is only pastoral propriety and discipline, in the second case the Church, by requiring absolute monogamy of the clergy, protects the scriptural, doctrinal and sacramental teaching on marriage. Thus, the main reason why a widowed priest cannot remarry—in spite of the personal tragedy which this prohibition may involve—is that the Church as a norm recognizes only one, eternal union of a husband and wife, and that she formally cannot but require that her priests maintain in their lives the norm which they must preach to others in virtue of their office. The firmness of the Orthodox Church on this particular point is the strongest witness to the fact that she remains faithful to the doctrine of marriage found in the New Testament, even if her "economy" and understanding do admit second and third marriages for laymen.

A later and purely disciplinary development of canon law reserves the episcopal rank to non-married men. This rule, first established by a state law of Emperor Justinian, is confirmed by the Quinisext (Sixth Ecumenical Council). Actually, the Council does not restrict the episcopate to celibates and admits the election of married men to this high ecclesiastical ministry, provided they separate from their wives: "The wife of him who is advanced to the episcopal dignity, shall be separated from her husband by their mutual consent, and after his ordination and consecration to the episcopate she shall enter a monastery situated at a distance from the abode of the bishop, and there let her enjoy the bishop's provision" (canon 48). Today, divorces by mutual consent, for the sake of the husband's elevation to the episcopate are—fortunately—extremely rare, and the general practice is to select the bishops from among priests who are either celibates or widowers. Earlier Church tradition knew many married bishops, still mentioned in Apostolic Canon 40. St. Gregory, bishop of Nyssa, brother of St. Basil the Great (late fourth century) and many contemporary bishops were married men.

Imperial legislation against ordaining married bishops was issued at a time when there was a large supply of celibate candidates and when a large number of monks constituted the elite of Christian society. It may also have been influenced by the belief that a bishop entered into a mystical marriage with his diocese and that his office required total dedication to the Church.

Today, the accepted canonical legislation on a non-married episcopate does greatly restrict the choice of new candidates. It is not sure, however, that a reform of the rule—attempted by the ill-fated "Renovated" schismatic group in Russia (1922)—would by itself guarantee the promotion of the best men to the episcopate. The present practice at least prevents the episcopal dignity from becoming simply the summit of ecclesiastical honors open to all clergy, and somehow preserves a charismatic principle of election. In any case, the possibility of returning to the ancient Christian practice and electing married men to the episcopate depends upon the decision of a new ecumenical council of the Orthodox Church, if it is ever held.

Whatever the pastoral and disciplinary restrictions established by the Church against marriage after ordination and in favor of a non-married episcopate, the general meaning of the Orthodox tradition is clear. Marriage is not an inferior state, but it is blessed by God. "Therefore," proclaims the Sixth Ecumenical Council, "if anyone shall have dared, contrary to the Apostolic canons, to deprive a priest, deacon,

or subdeacon, of cohabitation and intercourse with his legitimate wife, let him be deposed. In like manner also if any
presbyter or deacon has dismissed his wife on pretence of
piety, let him be deposed..." (canon 13; see also Council of
Gangra, canon 4). The problems faced today by the Roman
Church, where, for many centuries and on the basis of an
Augustinian concept of marriage, widely rejected today,
celibacy was imposed upon clergy, are unthinkable in Orthodoxy. Until quite recently, in Russia, parish duties were
formally reserved for married priests, while celibates, if they
were not living in a monastic community, could be appointed
only to educational or administrative posts in the Church. The
contemporary practice is generally more flexible, and many
celibate priests are successful parish pastors.

In any case, whatever the fluctuations in practice and
discipline, the Orthodox Church firmly holds married priesthood to be a positive norm of Church life, provided the
absolute principles of uniqueness and sacramentality of marriage are maintained.

XVI. MARRIAGE, CELIBACY
AND MONASTIC LIFE

One of the paradoxes of Christian ethics is that marriage
and celibacy, if they presuppose different practical behaviors,
are based on the same theology of the Kingdom of God and,
therefore, on the same spirituality.

We have seen in the beginning of this essay that the
peculiarity of Christian marriage consists in transforming and
transfiguring a natural human affection between a man and a
woman into an eternal bond of love, which cannot be broken
even by death. Marriage is a sacrament because in it the
future Kingdom of God—the marriage feast of the Lamb
(Rev. 19:7, 9), the full union between Christ and the
Church (Eph. 5:32)—is being anticipated and re-presented.
Christian marriage finds its ultimate meaning not in fleshly

satisfaction, or in social stability, or in securing posterity, but in the *eschaton,* the "last things" which the Lord prepares for His elect.

Now celibacy—and especially monastic life—is justified in Scripture and Tradition by the same reference to the future Kingdom. The Lord Himself has said that "when they rise from the dead, they neither marry nor are given in marriage, but are like angels in heaven" (Mark 12:25). We have seen above that this passage should not be understood to imply that Christian marriage will not remain a reality in the future Kingdom, but it certainly points to the fact that human relations will not be "fleshly" any more. Thus, the New Testament repeatedly praises celibacy as an anticipation of "angelic life": "There are eunuchs who have made themselves eunuchs for the sake of the Kingdom of heaven," says Christ (Matthew 19:12). The great figure of St. John the Baptist, that of St. Paul and the "hundred and forty-four thousand" mentioned in the Apocalypse (Rev. 14:3-4) served as models to innumerable Christian saints who practiced virginity for the glory of God.

Probably as a reaction against the sexual laxity prevailing in the pagan world, and also as an expression of the early Christian sense of the other-worldliness of Christianity, appeals to celibate life are very numerous in the writings of the Fathers of the Church. It seems even that monasticism appeared to many as the safe and highest solution of ethical problems. In spite of this predominance of the monastic spirit—which also expressed itself in the establishment of the unmarried episcopate—the Church maintained uncompromisingly the positive value of marriage. It also universally recognized in marriage a sacrament, while only some ecclesiastical writers attribute also a sacramental character to the ceremony of the monastic tonsure. This positive value of marriage is beautifully expressed in the extracts of Clement of Alexandria, one of the founders of Christian theology (third century), and of the great St. John Chrysostom (d. 407), reprinted below.

Thus, both marriage and celibacy are ways of living the Gospel, anticipating the Kingdom, which was already revealed in Christ and must appear in strength at the last day. It is, therefore, only a marriage "in Christ" sealed by the Eucharist, and celibacy "in the name of Christ," which carry this "eschatological" Christian meaning—not marriage concluded casually, as a contract, or as a satisfaction for the flesh, and not celibacy accepted by inertia, or worse, by egotism and self-protective irresponsibility.

Just as Christian marriage implies sacrifice, responsible family-building, dedication and maturity, so Christian celibacy is unthinkable without prayer, fasting, obedience, humility, charity and constant ascetical effort. Modern psychology did not *discover* the fact that the absence of sexual activity creates problems: the Fathers of the Church knew it very well, and elaborated a remarkable system of ascetical precepts—the basis of all monastic rules—which make purity possible and enjoyable. They knew, sometimes much better than modern psychologists, that the human instinct of love and procreation is not isolated from the rest of human existence, but is its very center. It cannot be suppressed, but only transformed, transfigured and channeled, as love for God and for one's neighbor, through prayer, fasting and obedience in the name of Christ. These virtues are codified and systematized in the monastic rules, but in different forms they also condition the Christian life of those who choose a celibate life of service in the world.

One of the major sources of the present trouble concerning clerical celibacy in the Roman Catholic Church is that the celibacy requirement is still enforced, but without the spirituality which used to serve as its natural setting, and without which it appears as unbearable and unnecessary. The breviary, the daily mass, the special "priestly" way of life in isolation from the world, poverty, fasting have now all been abandoned. The priest is not particularly limited in the natural satisfaction of his desires for food, drink, comfort, and money; and he does not follow any more any real discipline of prayer. His celibacy is then deprived of its spiritual significance, which can only be "eschatological"—directed towards the "Kingdom." How different from the "Kingdom" is the usually comfortable rectory, and how contradictory the appeals of modern theology towards "involvement in the world" and "social responsibility" as the only forms through which the Kingdom is to be revealed! Why, on earth, celibacy?

But, in Orthodoxy, celibacy practiced by some as a step towards episcopacy is, of course, an even worse spiritual danger. The entire tradition of the Church is absolutely unanimous in maintaining that authentic purity and monastic life can only be practiced in monastic communities. Only isolated and particularly strong personalities can practice a meaningful celibacy while living in the world. Humility is probably the only virtue which can really carry them through; but, as we all know, it is by far the most difficult and, therefore, the rarest of virtues.

The monastic tradition always has been recognized in Orthodoxy as the most authentic witness to the Gospel of Christ. As the prophets of the Old Testament, as the "martyrs" ("witnesses") of early Christianity, the monks made Christianity credible. By showing that one could lead a shining, joyful, meaningful life of prayer and service without being dependent upon the "normal conditions" of this world, they were giving a living proof that the Kingdom of God was indeed "in the midst" of us. The restoration of such a tradition would be particularly significant in the midst of our militantly secularized world. A humanity which pretends today that it "came of age" does not ask the help of Christianity in its quest for a "better world." It may, however, be interested in the Church again if the Church is able to manifest a world not only "better," but really *new and different.* This is what so many young people are looking for, but unfortunately discover only, at best, Zen Buddhism, but more frequently—psychedelics, and other means of escape towards . . . death.

Monks were the witnesses of this new world. If there had been more authentic monastic communities among us, our witness would have been stronger. However, Christ's *new creation* is also accessible to all of us, in all its beauty, through love in marriage, if only, with St. Paul, we accept it and understand it "in reference to Christ and the Church."

XVII. A WORD IN CONCLUSION

Marriage is a sacrament because in it and through it the Kingdom of God becomes a living experience. In each of the individual "sacraments," the same and unique Mystery of salvation becomes a reality and is applied to a concrete moment of human existence. Whether it is the entry into new life, the growth in the Spirit, the assumption of a Church ministry, the healing of disease, the same presence of the redeeming Christ is being conveyed through the Holy Spirit: in Baptism, in Chrismation, in the ordinations to the various degrees of priesthood, in the sacrament of the oil. And in each case, new life enters into the life of man—as a presence, not as an obligation, as a gift and a potential, not as magic; and man remains free to enter the door which is being opened in front of him, or to stay where he was in the realm of the "flesh."

However, all these individual "sacraments" receive their true reality and their meaning only if they lead to or express the corporate life of the Church, the Body of Christ. Baptism is an entrance into the Church; Chrismation is a gift which determines free growth in the Spirit; priesthood is a responsibility for the unity and the building up of the Body; the sacrament of oil bestows a new dimension of existence in the "new Adam," where there is no more disease or death. All these individual aspects of the life of the Body have their center and their fulfillment in the Mystery that makes the Church to be the Body of Christ: the Divine Liturgy of the Eucharist. Outside of the Body, there can be no "sacraments."

Now, the meaning of marriage, as sacrament, cannot be understood outside of this same eucharistic context. The Church, since its very early days, considered the legal or social institution of marriage as being transformed into a reality of the Kingdom, only if it was concluded between two members of the Body of Christ. It is in the flesh of Christ that two Christians can become flesh of each other in a truly Christian way. And it is in the Eucharist that they become Christians, by partaking of the Body of Christ. This is why, originally, marriages were blessed during the Divine Liturgy at which the bridegroom and the bride partook of Holy Communion. And this was possible only in the case of a first marriage, which both sides were able to accept as an eternal bond, indestructible by death itself.

This very sanctity of marriage, inasmuch as it involved human beings still living in a fallen and sickly world, needed the protection of legal rules and a few formal stipulations. We have seen that this formal, "canonical" side of the Church's practice is not, for the Church, an end in itself; it only indicates the ways through which the Christian ideal of a marriage, which is as unique as the union between Christ and the Church, can be best maintained in the conditions of our present world. It defines possible forms of toleration for imperfect forms of marriage—implying, in those cases, a separation between marriage and Eucharist—and protects the teaching and pastoral authority of the clerical state by excluding clerics from the tolerance granted to laymen.

By recognizing in marriage a mystery of the Kingdom of God, the Christian Gospel and the Church do not proclaim, however, a sort of mystic reality, detached from what man really is. The Christian faith is not only truth about God and His Kingdom, it is also truth about man. The Christian doctrine of marriage is, indeed, a joyful responsibility; it gives legitimate satisfaction to the soul and the body; it shows what it means to be truly man; it bestows upon man the ineffable joy of giving life, in the image of his Creator, who gave life to the first man.

To underline and express more fully the unity of the Orthodox tradition on marriage, we present, in appendices several fundamental scriptural texts on the meaning of marriage, and also passages written by saints or wise men of the past or of modern times. Their inspiration will give the true dimension to the liturgical and canonical texts which were quoted throughout the preceding chapters.

APPENDIX I

The New Testament

1. *The Resurrection changes the meaning of marriage*

LUKE 20:27-40.

There came to him some Sadducees, those who say that there is no resurrection, and they asked him a question, saying, "Teacher, Moses wrote for us that if a man's brother dies, having a wife but no children, the man must take the wife and raise up children for his brother. Now there were seven brothers; the first took a wife, and died without children; and the second and the third took her, and likewise all seven left no children and died. Afterwards the woman also died. In the resurrection, therefore, whose wife will the woman be? For the seven had her as wife."

And Jesus said to them, "The sons of this age marry and are given in marriage; but those who are accounted worthy to attain to that age and to the resurrection from the dead neither marry nor are given in marriage, for they cannot die any more, because they are equal to angels and are sons of God, being sons of the resurrection. But that the dead are raised, even Moses showed, in the passage about the bush, where he calls the Lord the God of Abraham and the God of Isaac and the God of Jacob. Now he is not God of the dead, but of the living; for all live to him. And some of the scribes

answered, "Teacher, you have spoken well." For they
no longer dared to ask him any question.

(See parallels in Matthew 22:23-32; Mark 12:18-27.)

2. *Divorce*

MATTHEW 5:31-32

It was also said, "Whoever divorces his wife, let him
give her a certificate of divorce" (Deut. 24:1-4). But
I say to you that everyone who divorces his wife except
on the ground of unchastity, makes her an adulteress;
and whoever marries a divorced woman commits adultery.

MATTHEW 19:3-12

And Pharisees came up to him and tested him by asking,
"Is it lawful to divorce one's wife for any cause?" He
answered, "Have you not read that he who made them
from the beginning made them male and female, and
said, 'For this reason a man shall leave his father and
mother and be joined to his wife, and the two shall
become one'? So they are no longer two but one. What
therefore God has joined together, let no man put
asunder." They said to him, "Why then did Moses
command one to give a certificate of divorce, and to put
her away?" He said to them, "For your hardness of
heart Moses allowed you to divorce your wives, but
from the beginning it was not so. And I say to you:
whoever divorces his wife, except for unchastity, and
marries another, commits adultery."

The disciples said to him, "If such is the case of a
man with his wife, it is not expedient to marry." But
he said to them, "Not all men can receive this precept,
but only those to whom it is given. For there are
eunuchs by men, and there are eunuchs for the sake
of the kingdom of heaven. He who is able to receive
this, let him receive it."

MARK 10:2-12

And Pharisees came up and in order to test him asked, "Is it lawful for a man to divorce his wife?" He answered them, "What did Moses command you?" They said, "Moses allowed a man to write a certificate of divorce, and to put her away." But Jesus said to them, "For your hardness of heart he wrote you this commandment. But from the beginning of creation, 'God made them male and female.' For this reason a man shall leave his father and mother and be joined to his wife, and the two shall become one. So they are no longer two but one. What therefore God has joined together, let no man put asunder."

And in the house the disciples asked him again about this matter. And he said to them, "Whoever divorces his wife and marries another, commits adultery against her; and if she divorces her husband and marries another, she commits adultery."

LUKE 16:-8

Everyone who divorces his wife and marries another commits adultery, and he who marries a woman divorced from her husband, commits adultery.

I COR. 7:10-16

To the married I give charge, not I but the Lord, that the wife should not separate from her husband (but if she does, let her remain single or else be reconciled to her husband)—and that the husband should not divorce his wife.

To the rest I say, not the Lord, that if any brother has a wife who is an unbeliever, and she consents to live with him, he should not divorce her.

If any woman has a husband who is an unbeliever, and he consents to live with her, she should not divorce him.

For the unbelieving husband is consecrated through

his wife, and the unbelieving wife is consecrated through her husband. Otherwise, your children would be unclean, but as it is they are holy. But if the unbelieving partner desires to separate, let it be so; in such a case the brother or sister is not bound. For God has called us to peace.

Wife, how do you know whether you will save your husband? Husband, how do you know whether you will save your wife?

3. *Jesus honors marriage by His presence*

JOHN 2:1-11

On the third day there was a marriage at Cana in Galilee, and the mother of Jesus was there; Jesus also was invited to the marriage, with his disciples. When the wine failed the mother of Jesus said to him, "They have no wine." And Jesus said to her, "O woman, what have you to do with me? My hour has not yet come." His mother said to the servants, "Do whatever he tells you." Now six stone jars were standing there, for the Jewish rites of purification, each holding twenty or thirty gallons. Jesus said to them, "Fill the jars with water." And they filled them up to the brim. He said to them, "Now draw some out, and take it to the steward of the feast." So they took it. When the steward of the feast tasted the water now become wine, and did not know where it came from (though the servants who had drawn the water knew), the steward of the feast called the bridegroom and said to him, "Every man serves the good wine first; and when men have drunk freely, then the poor wine; but you have kept the good wine until now." This, the first of his signs, Jesus did at Cana in Galilee, and manifested his glory; and his disciples believed in him.

4. Marriage—a "mystery"

EPH. 5:21-33

Be subject to one another out of reverence for Christ. Wives, be subject to your husbands, as to the Lord. For the husband is the head of the wife as Christ is the head of the church, his body, and is himself its Savior. As the church is subject to Christ, so let wives also be subject in everything to their husbands. Husbands, love your wives, as Christ loved the church and gave himself up for her, that he might sanctify her, having cleansed her by the washing of water with the word, that he might present the church to himself in splendor, without spot or wrinkle or any such thing, that she might be holy and without blemish.

Even so husbands should love their wives as their own bodies. He who loves his wife loves himself. For no man ever hates his own flesh, but nourishes and cherishes it, as Christ does the church, because we are members of his body. "For this reason a man shall leave his father and mother and be joined to his wife, and the two shall become one." This is a great mystery, and I take it to mean Christ and the church; however, let each one of you love his wife as himself, and let the wife see that she respects her husband.

5. Remarriage of widows

I COR. 7:39-40

A wife is bound to her husband as long as he lives. If the husband dies, she is free to be married to whom she wishes, only in the Lord. But in my judgment she is happier if she remains as she is. And I think that I have the Spirit of God.

APPENDIX II

The Tradition of the Church

1) St. John Chrysostom, Homily XX on Ephesians*

The meaning of love

"Husbands, love your wives, just as Christ (also) loved the Church." (Eph. 5:25)

You have heard of the magnitude of submission; you have praised and marvelled at Paul, how like an admirable and spiritual man, he welds together our whole life. You have done well. But now listen to what he requires from you in addition; he uses the same example again.

"Husbands," he says, "love your wives, just as Christ (also) loved the Church."

You have seen the amount of faithfulness necessary; now hear about the amount of love necessary. Do you want your wife to be obedient to you, as the Church is to Christ? Then take upon yourself the same providential care of her, as Christ takes upon Himself for the Church. And even if it becomes necessary for you to give your life for her, yes, and even to endure and undergo suffering of any kind,—do not refuse it. Even though

*English translation in Philip Schaff, ed., *A Select Library of the Nicene and Post-Nicene Fathers*, XIII, Grand Rapids, Mich., 1956, pp. 144-152.

you undergo all this, you will not, not even then, have done anything equal to what Christ has done. For you indeed are doing it for someone to whom you are already joined; but He did it for one who turned her back on Him, who hated, rejected, and disdained Him, not because of threats, or because of violence, or because of terror, or by anything else of this kind, but because of His untiring affection; so also should you behave towards your wife. Even though you see her looking down on you, and despising, and mocking you, still because of your great regard for her, through affection, through kindness, you will be able to lay her at your feet. For there is no influence more powerful than these bonds, and especially for husband and wife. A servant, indeed, one will be able, perhaps, to tie down by fear; no, not even him, for he will soon seek to escape and be gone. But the partner of one's life, the mother of one's children, the source of one's every joy one should never chain down by fear and threats, but with love and good temper. For what sort of union is it, where the wife is afraid of her husband? And what sort of satisfaction will the husband himself have, if he lives with his wife as if he were living with a slave, and not with a woman by her free will? Even though you would suffer anything on her account, do not chastize her, for neither did Christ do this.

Christ loved more

"And gave Himself up," he says, "for it, that He might sanctify and cleanse it." (Eph. 5:26)

So then she was not pure! So then she had blemishes, and she was ugly, so then she was worthless! Whatever kind of wife you take for yourself, you will never take a bride like the Church, when Christ took her; you would never take one so estranged from you as the Church was from Christ. And still for all that, He did not abhor her, nor loathe her for her extraordinary corruption. Do you want her corruption described? Saint Paul describes her: "For once you were in darkness." (Eph. 5:8) Did you see the blackness of her color? What is there blacker than darkness? But look again at her audacity, "living," says Paul, "in spite and envy." (Tit. 3:3) Look again at her impurity, "disobedient, foolish." But what am I saying? She was both foolish and caustic; and yet, even so, though her scars were so numerous, still He gave Himself up for her in her corrupted state, as if she were in the bloom of youth, as if she were a dearly loved one, as if she were a wonderful beauty. And it was out of admiration for this that Paul said, "For scarcely for a righteous man will one die" (Rom. 5:7); and again, "in that while we were still sinners, Christ died for us." (Rom. 5:8) And even though this was the situation, He took her, He showed her (the Church) in beauty, and He washed her, and did not refuse even the giving of Himself for her.

What is true beauty?

"That He might sanctify it having cleansed it," he continues, "by the washing of water with the word; that He might present the Church to Himself a glorious Church, not having spot, or wrinkle, or any such thing, but that it should be holy and without blemish." (Eph. 5:26-27)

"By the washing or laver," He washes away her impurities. "By the word," says he. What word? "In the name of the Father and of the Son, and of the Holy Spirit." (Matt. 28:19) And He has not simply honored her, but He has made her "glorious, not having spot or wrinkle, or any such thing." Let us also, then, strive to attain this beauty ourselves, and we shall be able to create it. Do not look in your wife for those things which she is unable to possess. Do you see that the Church had all things at her Lord's hands? By Him she was made glorious, by Him she was made pure, by Him she was made without blemish. Do not turn your back on your wife because of her defects. Listen to what the Scripture says, that "The bee is little among such as fly, but her fruit is the chief of sweet things." (Eccl. 11:3) She is made by God. You are not condemning her, but rather the One who made her; what can the woman do? Do not praise her for her beauty. Praise and hatred and love based on personal beauty come from impure souls. Search after the beauty of the soul. Imitate the Bridegroom of the Church. Outward beauty is full of conceit and licentiousness, and makes men jealous, and it often makes you imagine monstrous things. But does it give any pleasure? For the first or second month, perhaps, or at most, for the year: but then no longer. The admiration fades away through familiarity. Meanwhile the ills which arose from the exterior beauty still remain; the pride, the foolishness, the contemptuousness. However, in one who is not beautiful, none of this is to be found. The love that began on honest grounds still continues ardently, since its object is beauty of the soul and not of the body. What better, tell me, is there than heaven? What better is there than the stars? Describe any body you choose, and still there is none so fair. Tell me of any eyes you want, yet there are none so sparkling. When these were created, the very angels gazed in amazement, and we gaze with wonder now; but not with the same amazement as we did at first. Such familiarity; things do not strike us in the same degree. How much more in the case of the wife! And if by some chance disease comes, too, all is immediately lost. Look for affection, humility, and gentleness in a wife; these are the signs of beauty. But loveliness of physical features let us not seek, nor chastize her for lack of these points over which she has no control. No, rather let us not chastize her at all nor be be impatient, nor morose. Don't you see how many men, often living with beautiful wives, have ended their lives despicably, and how many, who have lived with those of no great beauty, have lived on to extreme old age with great enjoyment? Let us wipe off the "spot" that is written, let us smooth the "wrinkles" that are within, let us do away with the "blemishes" that are on the soul. Such is the beauty God requires. Let us make her fair in God's sight not in our own.

Money corrupts

Let us not look for wealth, nor for that high social position (which is external), but for that true nobility which is in the soul. Let no one exist for the purpose of getting rich by a wife; such wealth is base and disgraceful; no, by no means let anyone aspire to get rich from this source. "For they that desire to be rich fall into a temptation and a snare, and many foolish and harmful lusts, and into destruction and perdition." (I Timothy 6:9) Do not look in your wife for great wealth, and you will find that everything else will go well. Who, tell me, would overlook the most important things to turn attention to the secondary matters? And yet, to our sorrow, that is our desire in every case. Yes, if we have a son, we worry about how we might find him a rich wife, and not about how he might develop a virtuous nature; nor about how he might develop into a well-mannered person, but how he might become well-monied: if we engage in business, we do not think about how it might be free from sin, but how it might bring in the most profit. Everything has become money, and therefore everything is corrupted and ruined, because that passion for money possesses us.

Nothing can be better...

"Nevertheless each one of you individually love your own wives as you love your own selves; and the wife should be sure that she respects her husband." (Eph. 5:33)

For indeed, of all actions, it is a mystery, in fact, a great mystery, that a man should leave him who gave life to him and that brought him up, and her who suffered in birth and was pained, leave those who have graced him with so many and great benefits, those with whom he has been in close contact, and be united to one who was never even known to him and who has nothing in common with him, and should honor her higher than all others. It is a mystery indeed. And yet parents are not distressed when these things take place, but when they do not take place! They are delighted when their money is spent and lavished upon it.—A great mystery indeed! And one that contains some hidden wisdom. Moses prophetically showed this to be so from the very first; so does Paul now proclaim it, where he says "concerning Christ and the Church."

However, this is not said for the sake of the husband alone, but for the wife's sake also, that "he cherish her as his own flesh, as Christ also the Church," and, "that the wife respects her husband." He is no longer setting down the duties of love only, but what? That she fear her husband. The wife is a second authority; she should not demand equality, for she is under the head; neither should the husband have contempt for her as if she were in subjection, for she is the body. And if the head despises the body, it will itself die. But rather let him bring in love on his part to counterbalance obedience on her part. For example, let the hands and the feet, and all the rest of the parts of the body be dedicated to the service of the head, but let the head provide for the body, seeing to it that it contains reason in itself. Nothing can be better than this union . . .

Second marriage a concession

But what will those who are joined in second marriages say? I don't speak in condemnation of them, no not at all; God forbid! for the Apostle Paul himself permits them, though indeed he does it as a concession.

The little church

Supply her with everything. Do everything and put up with troubles for her sake. The necessity of the situation is put on you. Here he (Paul) does not think it appropriate to bring advice by way of examples from outside sources, as he does in many cases. That (wisdom) of Christ, so great and forceful, was alone enough; and especially this is true in regard to subjection (of the wife). "A man should leave," he says, "his father and mother." You see, this is an outside example. But he does not say, and "shall dwell with," but instead says "shall cling to," thus demonstrating the closeness of the union, and the sincerity of the love. No, he is not satisfied with this, but goes further, even, by what he adds to explain the subjection (of the wife) in such a way so as the two are no longer two. He does not say "one spirit;" he does not say "one soul" (for this is already revealed and is possible to any one); but he says be "one flesh." She (the wife) is a second authority, possessing, in fact, another authority and a considerable equality of dignity; but at the same time the husband has somewhat the role of the superior. In this, the well-being of the household is found. For Paul took that other argument, the example of Christ, to show that we should not only love, but also govern; "that she may be," says Paul "holy and without blemish." But the word "flesh" is used with reference to love—and the phrase "shall cling" has, likewise, reference to love. For if you make her "holy and without blemish" everything else will follow. Seek the things which belong to God, and those that belong to man will follow soon enough. Instruct your wife, and the whole of your household will be in order and harmony. Hear what Paul says. "And if they (the wives) desire to learn anything, let them ask their own husbands at home about it." (I Cor. 14:35) If we regulate our households in this manner, we will also be fit for the management of the Church. For indeed the household is a little Church. Therefore, it is possible for us to surpass all others (in our accomplishments and esteem) by becoming good husbands and wives . . .

"My own": a cursed phrase

If you are inclined to entertain and give dinner parties, there should be nothing disorderly or immodest about them. And if you should find some poor, saintly man who just by stepping his foot into your house would bring in the whole blessing of God, invite him. And I'll add one more thing. None of you should strive to marry a rich woman, but rather a poor one. When she comes in she will not bring such great satisfaction from her own money, since she will annoy you with her taunts, if she be rich, and with her demands for more than she brought with her, with her disrespect, her extravagance, her frustrating manner of speaking. Because she might say, "I haven't spent anything of yours yet; I am still wearing my own clothes bought with the inheritance given to me by my parents." What are you saying, woman? Still wearing your own! And what can be more terrible than this sort of language? Why, you no longer have a body of your own (since it was given to a union through marriage) and you have money of your own? After marriage, you are no longer two, but have become one flesh, and are your possessions still two, and not of the oneness? This love of money! You have both become one person, one living creature, and you can still say "my own"? That cursed and abominable phrase was brought in by the devil. Things that are far nearer and dearer to us than these (material considerations) God has made common to both; are these, then, not also common now? We cannot say "my own light, my own sun, my own water": all our greater blessings are common, and should money not be common? Let the riches be lost ten thousand times over! Or rather, not let the riches be lost, but that frame of mind that doesn't know how to make use of money, and holds it higher in esteem than all other things.

Teach her these lessons along with the rest (I have indicated), but do it with much compassion. For because the direction of a virtuous life has in itself much that is difficult to follow, and is especially difficult for a young and innocent lady, whenever you have to lecture her on the true wisdom, be sure that you humble yourself and that your manner is full of grace and kindness. And above all, remove from her soul this notion of "mine and yours." If she says the word "mine," ask her "What things do you call yours? Because, in reality, I don't know (what these things are); I, for my part, have nothing of my own. How, then, can you speak of 'mine' when all things are yours?" But let her speak freely and say these things. Do you understand that we employ the same practice with children? While we are holding anything, when a child snatches it away, and wants to get hold of something else yet, we allow it, and say "Yes, this is yours and that is yours." Do the same also with a wife; for her temper is more or less like a child's. And if she says "mine," then say, "Why yes everything is yours, and I am yours." This expression isn't meant to flatter, but it is full of wisdom. You will be able to subside her wrath, and end her disappointment. It is flattery when a man acts dishonorably with an evil motive in mind; this, however, is the most honorable of motivations. Say this (to her), then, "Even I am yours, my child." St. Paul gives this advice when he says, "The husband does not have power over his own body, but the wife (has power over it)." (I Cor. 7:4) "If I have no power over my own body, but rather you do, how much more power is yours over my material possessions." By saying these things, you will placate her, you will have subsided her anger, you will have shamed the devil, you will make her more your servant than if you had bought a servant with money, and with this language you will firmly unite her to you. In this manner will you teach her, by your own manner of speaking, never to speak in terms of "mine and yours."

Teaching of love

And again, never call her by her name alone, but with terms of endearment also, with honor, with much love. If you honor her, she won't require honor from others; she won't desire that praise that others give if she enjoys the praise that comes from you. Prefer her before all others, in every way, both for her beauty and for her sensitivity, and praise her. You will in this way persuade her to listen to none that are outside (of your union with one another), but to disregard all the world except for you. Teach her to fear God, and all good things will flow from this lesson as from a fountain, and your house will be filled with ten thousand blessings. If we seek the things that are perfect, these imperfect (and secondary things) will follow. "For," says the Lord, "seek first His Kingdom, and all these things shall be added to you." (Matt. 6:33) What sort of person do you think the children of such parents will be? What kind of servants under such masters; what kind of person all the others who associate with them? Will they not, too, eventually be the recipients of countless blessings? For generally the servants acquire the character of their master, and are formed in the mold of their master's temperament, love the same things, which they have been taught to love, talk in the same fashion, and engage in the same endeavors. If we direct ourselves in this manner, and diligently study the Scriptures, in most things we will find lessons to guide us in them. And in this way we will be able to please God, and to pass through the whole of this life in virtue, and to gain those blessings which are promised to those that love Him, of which, God willing, we may be counted worthy, through the grace and lovingkindness of our Lord Jesus Christ, with Whom, together with the Holy Spirit, be to the Father, glory, power, and honor, now and ever through all ages. Amen.

2)   Clement of Alexandria

Miscellanies, or *Stromateis,* Book III (tr. by J. E. L. Oulton and H. Chadwick in *The Library of Christian Classics,* II, Philadelphia, The Westminster Press, 1954)

Marriage and celibacy

Continence is an ignoring of the body in accordance with the confession of faith in God. For continence is not merely a matter of sexual abstinence, but applies also to the other things for which the soul has an evil desire because it is not satisfied with the necessities of life. There is also a continence of the tongue, of money, of use, and of desire. It does not only teach us to exercise self-control; it is rather that self-control is granted to us, since it is divine power and grace. Accordingly I must declare what is the opinion of our people about this subject. Our view is that we welcome as blessed the state of abstinence from marriage in those to whom this has been granted by God. We admire monogamy and the high standing of single marriage, holding that we ought to share suffering with another and "bear one another's burdens,"[22] lest anyone who thinks he stands securely should himself fall.[23] It is of second marriage that the apostle says, If you burn, marry.[24] (tr. cit., pp. 41-42)

Sanctification of the body and soul

In us it is not only the spirit which ought to be sanctified, but also our behavior, manner of life, and our body. What does the apostle Paul mean when he says that the wife is sanctified by the husband and the husband by the wife?[25] And what is the meaning of the Lord's words to those who asked concerning divorce

[22]Gal. 6:2
[23]I Cor. 10:12
[24]I Cor. 7:9
[25]I Cor. 7:14

whether it is lawful to put away one's wife as Moses
commanded? "Because of the hardness of your hearts,"
he says, "Moses wrote this; but have you not read that
God said to the first man, You two shall be one flesh?
Therefore he who divorces his wife except for fornication makes her an adulteress."[26] But "after the resurrection," he says, "they neither marry nor are given in
marriage."[27] Moreover, concerning the belly and its
food it is written: "Food is for the belly and the belly
for food; but God shall destroy both the one and the
other."[28] In this saying he attacks those who think they
can live like wild pigs and goats, lest they should indulge
their physical appetites without restraint.

If, as they say, they have already attained the state
of resurrection, and on this account reject marriage let
them neither eat nor drink. For the apostle says that in
the resurrection the belly and food shall be destroyed.
Why then do they hunger and thirst and suffer the
weaknesses of the flesh and all the other needs which
will not affect the man who through Christ has attained
to the hoped for resurrection? Furthermore those who
worship abstain both from food and from sexual intercourse. "But the kingdom of God does not consist in
eating and drinking,"[29] he says. And indeed the Magi
make a point of abstaining from wine and the meat of
animals and from sexual intercourse while they are
worshipping angels and demons. But just as humility
consists in meekness and not in treating one's body
roughly, so also continence is a virtue of the soul which
is not manifest to others, but is in secret.

There are some who say outright that marriage is
fornication and teach that it was introduced by the devil.
They proudly say that they are imitating the Lord who
neither married nor had any possession in this world,
boasting that they understand the gospel better than
anyone else. The Scripture says to them: "God resists

[26]Matt. 19:3-9
[27]Matt. 22:30
[28]I Cor. 6:13
[29]Rom. 14:17

the proud but gives grace to the humble."[30] Further, they do not know the reason why the Lord did not marry. In the first place he had his own bride, the Church; and in the next place he was no ordinary man that he should also be in need of some helpmeet[31] after the flesh. Nor was it necessary for him to beget children since he abides eternally and was born the only Son of God. It is the Lord himself who says: "That which God has joined together, let no man put asunder."[32] And again: "As it was in the days of Noah, they were marrying, and giving in marriage, building and planting, and as it was in the days of Lot, so shall be the coming of the Son of man."[33] And to show that he is not referring to the heathen he adds: "When the Son of man is come, shall he find faith on the earth?"[34] And again: "Woe to those who are with child and are giving suck in those days,"[35] a saying, I admit, to be understood allegorically. The reason why he did not determine "the times which the Father has appointed by his own power"[36] was that the world might continue from generation to generation. (tr. cit., pp. 62-63)

Responsible parenthood

Our general argument concerning marriage, food, and other matters, may proceed to show that we should do nothing from desire. Our will is to be directed only towards that which is necessary. For we are children not of desire but of will.[37] A man who marries for the sake of begetting children must practise continence so that it is not desire he feels for his wife, whom he ought to love, and that he may beget children with a chaste and controlled will. For we have learnt not to "have thought

[30]James 4:6; I Peter 5:5
[31]Gen. 2:18
[32]Matt. 19:6
[33]Matt. 24:37-39
[34]Luke 18:8
[35]Matt. 24:18
[36]Acts 1:7
[37]Cf. John 1:13

for the flesh to fulfil its desires." We are to "walk honorably as in the way," that is in Christ and in the enlightened conduct of the Lord's way "not in revelling and drunkenness, not in debauchery and lasciviousness, not in strife and envy."[38]

However, one ought to consider continence not merely in relation to one form of it, that is, sexual relations, but in relation to all the other indulgences for which the soul craves when it is ill content with what is necessary and seeks for luxury. It is continence to despise money, softness, property, to hold in small esteem outward appearance, to control one's tongue, to master evil thoughts. In the past certain angels became incontinent and were seized by desire so that they fell from heaven to earth.[39] (tr. cit., p. 67)

Whether a man becomes a celibate or whether he joins himself in marriage with a woman for the sake of having children, his purpose ought to be to remain unyielding to what is inferior. If he can live a life of intense devotion, he will gain himself great merit with God, since continence is both pure and reasonable. But if he goes beyond the rule he has chosen to gain greater glory, there is a danger that he may lose hope. Both celibacy and marriage have their own different forms of service and ministry to the Lord; I have in mind the caring for one's wife and children. For it seems that the particular characteristic of the married state is that it gives the man who desires a perfect marriage an opportunity to take responsibility for every thing in the home which he shares with his wife. The apostle says that one should appoint bishops who by their oversight over their own house have learned to be in charge of the whole church.[40] Let each man therefore fulfill his ministry by the work in which he was called,[41] that he

[38]Rom. 13:13-14
[39]Gen. 6:2
[40]I Tim. 3:4f
[41]I Cor. 7:24

may be free[42] in Christ and receive the proper reward of his ministry. (tr. cit., pp. 76-77)

Celibacy can be irresponsible

For the fear of the Lord is said to be the beginning of wisdom.[43] But he that is perfect beareth all things and endureth all things[44] for love's sake, not as pleasing man, but God.[45] Yet praise too attends him by way of natural consequence, not for his own benefit, but for the imitation and use of those who bestow that praise. The word meaning continent is used in another sense also, not of him who only conquers his passions, but of him also who has become possessed of good and has a firm hold of the treasures of understanding, from which spring the fruits of virtuous activity. Thus the gnostic never departs from his own set habit in any emergency. For the scientific possession of good is fixed and unchangeable, being the science of things divine and human. Knowledge therefore never becomes ignorance, nor does good change to evil. Hence with him eating and drinking and marrying are not the main objects of life, though they are its necessary conditions. I speak of marriage sanctioned by reason and in accordance with right: for being made perfect he has the apostles as his patterns. And true manhood is shown not in the choice of a celibate life; on the contrary the prize in the contest of men is won by him who has trained himself by the discharge of the duties of husband and father and by the supervision of a household, regardless of pleasure and pain—by him, I say, who in the midst of his solicitude for his family shows himself inseparable from the love of God and rises superior to every temptation which assails him through children and wife and servants and possessions. On the other hand he who has no family is in most respects untried. In any case, as he takes thought only

[42]I Cor. 7:22
[43]Prov. 9:10
[44]I Cor. 13:7
[45]I Thess. 2:4

for himself, he is inferior to one who falls short of him as regards his own salvation, but who has the advantage in the conduct of life, inasmuch as he actually preserves a faint image of the true Providence.

3) Father Alexander Elchaninov (1881-1934)*

Marriage or monasticism

There is the monastic life and the state of marriage. The third condition, that of virginity in the world, is extremely dangerous, fraught with temptation, and beyond the strength of most people. Moreover, those who adhere to this condition are also a danger to the persons around them: the aura and beauty of virginity, which, when deprived of direct religious significance, are in a sense "nuptial feathers," exercise a powerful attraction and awaken unedifying emotions. (p. 45)

Marriage transforms

Marriage is a revelation and a mystery. We see in it the complete transformation of a human being, the expansion of his personality, fresh vision, a new perception of life, and through it a rebirth into the world in a new plenitude.

Our modern individualism creates special difficulties in married life. To overcome them, a conscious effort on both sides is necessary, in order to build up the marriage and make it a "walking in the presence of God." (The Church alone provides a full and genuine solution for

---

*A Russian priest, living in France, Father Alexander Elchaninov was recognized as a remarkable spiritual director. He was particularly loved by young people. His diary was published after his death by his widow, Tamara Elchaninov. Quotations are from the recent English edition, *The Diary of a Russian Priest,* translated by Helen Iswolsky. English edition prepared by Kallistos Timothy Ware, with an introduction by Tamara Elchaninov and a Foreword by Dimitri Obolensky, SVS Press, Crestwood, NY, 1982.

all problems.) And there is something further, something which may appear to be the simplest thing of all, but which is nevertheless the most difficult to achieve—a firm intention to allow each partner to preserve his or her proper place in the marriage—for the wife humbly to assume the second place, for the husband to take up the burden and the responsibility of being the head. If this firm intention and desire are present, God will always help us to follow this difficult path, the path of martyrdom—the chant of the "Holy martyrs" is sung in the course of the bridal procession—but also a way of life that yields the most intense joy.

Marriage, fleshly love, is a very great sacrament and mystery. Through it is accomplished the most real and at the same time the most mysterious of all possible forms of human relationship. And, qualitatively, marriage enables us to pass beyond all the normal rules of human relationship and to enter a region of the miraculous, the superhuman.

In fleshly love, besides its intrinsic value as such, God has granted the world a share in His omnipotence: man creates man, a new soul is brought into being.

Full dimension of life

Man enters deeply into the texture of the world through his family alone.

Neither the man (still less) the woman, possesses absolute power over the other partner in the marriage. Coercion exercised over the will of another—even in the name of love—kills love itself. And so the question arises: must one submit to coercion if it threatens that which is most precious? A countless number of unhappy marriages result from precisely this—that each partner considers him or herself as the owner of the loved one. This is the cause of nearly all the difficulties of married life. The highest wisdom in marriage is shown by giving full freedom to the person you love: for our human marriage is the counterpart of the marriage in heaven between Christ and the Church, where there is absolute freedom.

Woman has been called the "weaker vessel." This "weakness" consists especially in her enslavement to the natural, elemental forces within and outside herself. The result is inadequate self-control, irresponsibility, passionateness, blindness in judgment. Scarcely any woman is free from all these defects; she is always the slave of her passions, of her dislikes, of her desires. In Christianity alone does woman become man's equal, submitting her temperament to higher principles, and so acquiring moderation, patience, the ability to think rationally, wisdom. Only then does friendship with the husband become possible.

How sad and incomplete maidenhood is, and what a plenitude of life is found in womanhood. No love affair is capable of replacing marriage. In love affairs people are seen in their splendor and blossoming, yet they are themselves: a love affair projects a deceptive, exaggerated image of reality, and the life of both lovers is inevitably a pose, though an excusable and innocent one.

Only in marriage can human beings fully know one another—the miracle of feeling, touching, seeing another's personality—and this is as wonderful and as unique as the mystic's knowledge of God. It is for this reason that before marriage man hovers above life, observing it from without; only in marriage does he plunge into it, entering it through the personality of another. This delight in real knowledge and real life gives us a feeling of achieved plenitude and satisfaction which makes us richer and wiser.

Children

And this fullness is made still deeper through the emergence from the two of us—fused and reconciled—of a third, our child.

But from this arise unsurmountable difficulties: instead of a complex fulness, there usually appears a mutual misunderstanding, protests, and an almost inevitable separation of that third one from us. The couple cannot become a perfect trinity. Why should this be so? Is this failure inevitable? Can we do anything to prevent it from happening? That which we have procreated is part of ourselves, our flesh and blood and soul. In a child we recognize our own habits, inclinations—whence then the disagreement, the breaking away? I think that a perfect couple will produce a perfect child, which will continue to develop further according to the laws of perfection. But if in the married life of the couple there is an unresolved conflict, a contradiction, the child will be the offspring of this contradiction and will prolong it. If we have reconciled our antagonism only externally and have not conquered it by rising to a new level, this will be reflected in the child.

Another explanation: in the child, together with the soul and body which it has received from us, there is something further, which is essential—a unique and inimitable personality with its own way of life.

In the education of children, the most important thing is that they should see their parents leading an intense interior life.

Family problems

The philosophy of family quarrels: they often result from the wife's reproaches, borne reluctantly by the husband even though they may be deserved (pride). It is necessary to discover the original cause of these reproaches. They often come from the wife's desire to see her husband better than he is in reality, from her asking too much, that is to say from a kind of idealization. On these occasions, the wife becomes her husband's conscience and he should accept her rebukes as such. A man tends, especially in marriage, to let things slip, to be content with empirical facts. The wife tears him away from this and expects something more from her husband. In this sense, family discords, strange as it may seem, are proof that the marriage has been fulfilled (not only planned): and in the new human being, in which two persons have merged, the wife plays the role of conscience.

That is why quarrels between people who are close to each other are on occasion even useful: the fire of the quarrel burns up all the rubbish of resentment and misunderstanding, sometimes accumulated over a long period. A mutual explanation and confession is followed by a feeling of complete calm and serenity—everything has been clarified, nothing weighs on our mind. Then the highest gifts of the soul are freed; entering into communion with one another, we come to talk over the most wonderful things, we reach a full unity of soul and mind.

Love is a feast

In marriage the festive joy of the first day should last for the whole of life; every day should be a feast day; every day husband and wife should appear to each other as new, extraordinary beings. The only way of achieving this: let both deepen their spiritual life, and strive hard in the task of self-development.

So precious in marriage is love alone, so dreadful is it to lose love—and sometimes it vanishes because of such trifles—that we must direct all our thoughts and efforts toward this goal (also toward the "Divine"). Everything else will come by itself.

Outline of a sermon on marriage

Thesis: Marriage is an institution blessed by God: Cana of Galilee, "be fruitful and multiply" (Gen. i. 28), the sacrament of marriage, the wedding ceremony. Everything is all right.

Antithesis: "It is good for them if they abide even as I" (Cor. vii. 8); the hundred and forty and four thousand virgins "which were redeemed from the earth" and "were not defiled with women" (Rev. xiv. 3-4); "eunuchs for the kingdom of heaven's sake" (Matt. xix.

12); absence of saints glorified for their family virtues.

Synthesis (but not a full one, for nothing is yet fulfilled for us, all is infected by sin, including matrimony): Adam and Eve were created before the fall; the "Song of Songs"; the symbolism of the Gospel: "the marriage feast," the bridegroom and the bride—Christ and the Church, "this is a great mystery." (Eph. v. 32)

APPENDIX III

Canon Law

Orthodox Canon Law is based on a collection of ancient texts, reflecting the discipline and practice of the first millennium of Christian history. They are:

—the canons of the Seven Ecumenical Councils,

—the rules issued by certain local or provincial Councils which later received universal acceptance, and

—the canons of the Fathers, i.e., a collection of advice and precepts issued by individual Fathers of the Church and endorsed by the Councils.

The Sixth Ecumenical Council (canon 2) also endorses, as authoritative, a collection of 85 "Apostolic canons," representing the discipline of the Church of Antioch in the fourth century.

Most of these texts can be found in English translation (see *Nicene and Post-Nicene Fathers*, vol. XIV, Wm. B. Eerdmans Publishing Company, Grand Rapids, Mich., n.d.).

They constitute the foundation of all modern statutes and by-laws, adopted today by the various Orthodox Patriarchates and autocephalous churches. In countries where Orthodoxy was, or is, an established religion, the State also accepted them as guiding principles of its own legislation.

Even the most superficial reading of these canonical

texts reveals that they are neither a system, nor a code, but rather occasional rules on various issues of Christian life. Some of them refer to situations which have no rapport with the world of today. Others deal with eternal values and must, therefore, remain as basic criteria for our own life. The Church and, more particularly, the bishops have the responsibility for interpreting and applying the canons to contemporary issues as they arise.

As "column and foundation of Truth," the Church must remain always consistent with itself in proclaiming and defending the Truth, which is eternal and unchangeable. But the *means* of expressing and protecting it do inevitably change in a changing world. This is why some canonical texts may lose their binding importance, when the Church considers that the Truth or the social values which these texts were once expressing, can be protected better in a different way. For example, no one would claim today that canon 54 of the Sixth Ecumenical Council, forbidding the marriage of two brothers with two sisters, is to be strictly applied, since it obviously reflects social ideas of another age and does not involve any permanent value of either divine, or human nature. Updating and revision of irrelevant canons is on the agenda of the forthcoming Council of the Orthodox Church.

Meanwhile, the Church must interpret the canons in their present form. In doing so, she has always in mind *the basic elements of the Christian faith*: it is only in so far as they reflected the faith that canons have permanent authority. And indeed, many of them were issued precisely in order to express this faith, and cannot be treated lightly.

The Orthodox Church is generally quite strict in applying the ancient rules to members of the clergy, who are called to preach the Gospel to others not only in words, but also by the example of their lives. For laymen it frequently uses the principle of "economy" (or "management"), condescending to human circumstances and understanding difficult situations.

We are giving below a selection of canonical texts which illustrate the Church's attitude towards questions related to marriage.

1. *Marriage is honorable*

If anyone shall condemn marriage..., let him be anathema (Council of Gangra, canon 1).

If anyone shall remain virgin, or observe continence, abstaining from marriage because he abhors it, and not on account of the beauty and holiness of virginity itself, let him be anathema (same council, canon 9).

If anyone of those who are living a virgin life for the Lord's sake shall treat arrogantly the married, let him be anathema (same council, canon 10).

If any woman shall forsake her husband and resolve to depart from him because she abhors marriage, let her be anathema (same council, canon 14).

2. *Unity of faith: a prerequisite*

An orthodox man is not permitted to marry an heretical woman, nor an orthodox woman to be joined to an heretical man. But if anything of this kind appear to have been done by any, we require them to consider the marriage null, and that the marriage be dissolved... But if any who up to this time are unbelievers and are not yet numbered in the flock of the orthodox have contracted lawful marriage between themselves, and if then, one choosing the right and coming to the light of truth and the other remaining still detained by the bond of error...., the unbelieving woman is pleased to cohabit with the believing man, or the unbelieving man with the believing woman, let them not be separated, according to the divine Apostle, "for the unbelieving husband is sanctified by the wife, and the unbelieving wife by her husband" (I Cor. 7:13-15). (Sixth Ecumenical Council, canon 72).

3. *Successive marriages discouraged*

The rule establishes one year of excommunication for those who marry a second time. Other authorities even require two years. Those who marry a third time are often excommunicated for three or four years. And such marriages are to be considered as polygamy, and even as fornication ... So that one should not admit such people into the Church immediately, but, for two or three years admit them to hear the service (together with the catechumens), but make them abstain from communion. Only when they will show fruits of repentance, shall they be restored to communion (St. Basil the Great, canon 4).

A second marriage is not crowned in Church, but the couple is prevented from receiving the immaculate Mysteries for two years; in case of a third marriage, there is five years excommunication (St. Nicephorus the Confessor, Patriarch of Constantinople, canon 2).

We declare, by common opinion and judgment, that, beginning this year 920, no one will dare to enter into a fourth marriage, and that if anyone will desire such a cohabitation, he will be excluded from every church celebration and will not even be permitted to enter the holy temple, as long as he remains in the said cohabitation ... Also, condescending to human weakness ..., we decree the following concerning third marriages:

—if a man has reached the age of forty and wants to marry a third time, let him do so, but he shall abstain from communion for five years, and even then he will not approach communion at any time except only on the day of the saving Resurrection of Christ our God (Easter Day). And we issue this rule for those who did not have children from previous marriages, but if they had children, a third marriage after the age of forty is not permissible.

—if a man is aged 30, has children from previous marriages and wants to marry a third time, let him abstain from communion for four years, and then be worthy of the sacraments three times a year only: once on the Day of the saving Resurrection of Christ our God; a second time on the Dormition of our immaculate Lady Theotokos, and a third time on the Nativity of Christ our God. If he had no children, and since it is a good thing to desire children, the third marriage will be forgiven under the penitential rules established so far (Council of Constantinople, 920, also known as "Tome of Union"; simplified translation from the Greek).*

4. *Remarriage after divorce requires penance*

She who has left her husband is an adulteress if she has come to another ... If therefore she appears to have departed from her husband without reason, he is deserving of pardon and she of punishment. And pardon shall be given to him that he may be in communion with the Church. But he who leaves the wife lawfully given him, and shall take another is guilty of adultery by the sentence of the Lord. And it has been decreed by our Fathers that they who are such must be "weepers" for a year, "hearers" for two years, "prostrators" for three years, and in the seventh year to stand with the faithful and thus be counted worthy of the Oblation (Sixth Ecumenical Council, canon 87).

5. *Married Priesthood*

If anyone shall maintain, concerning a married priest, that it is not lawful to partake of the oblation when he offers it, let him be anathema (Council of Gangra, canon 4).

Since we know it to be handed down as a rule of the Roman church that those who are deemed worthy to be advanced to the diaconate or the priesthood should promise no longer to live with their wives, we, preserving

---

*The full critical text of the "Tome of Union" has been published by L. G. Westerink, *Nicholas I Patriarch of Constantinople, Miscellaneous Writings,* Washington, DC, 1981, pp. 58-69.

the ancient and apostolic perfection and order, will that the lawful marriages of men who are in holy orders be from this time forward firm, by no means dissolving their union with their wives, nor depriving them of their mutual intercourse at a convenient time. Wherefore, if anyone shall have been found worthy to be ordained subdeacon, or deacon, or priest, he is by no means to be prohibited from admittance to such a rank, if he shall live with his wife ... lest we should affect injuriously marriage constituted by God and blessed by His presence, as the Gospel says: "What God has joined together let no man put asunder" (Matt. 19:6); and the Apostle says: "Marriage is honorable and the bed undefiled" (Heb. 13:4); and again: "Are you bound to a wife? Seek not to be loosed" (I Cor. 7:27) (Sixth Ecumenical Council, canon 13).

6. No successive marriages possible for priests or their wives

He who has been twice married after baptism, or who has had a concubine, cannot become a bishop, priest or deacon, or a member of the clergy altogether (Apostolic canon 17).

He who married a widow, or a divorced woman, or an harlot, or a slave, or an actress,[46] cannot become a bishop, a priest, a deacon, or a member of the clergy altogether (Apostolic canon 18).

7. Members of the clergy cannot marry after their ordination

Of those who have been admitted to the clergy unmarried, we ordain that the readers and singers only may, if they wish, marry (Apostolic canon 26).

If a priest marry, let him be removed from his order ... (Council of Neocaesarea, canon 1).

Since it is declared in the apostolic canons that of those who are advanced to the clergy unmarried, only readers and singers are able to marry, we also, maintain-

---

[46]In the ancient world, promiscuous life was considered inevitable for slaves and actors.

ing this, determine that henceforth it is in nowise lawful for any subdeacon, deacon or priest, after his ordination, to contract matrimony. But if he shall have dared to do so, let him be deposed. And if any of those who enter the clergy wishes to be joined to a wife in lawful marriage before he is ordained subdeacon, deacon or priest, let it be done (Sixth Ecumenical Council, canon 6).

8. *Unmarried bishops*

The wife of him who is advanced to the episcopal dignity shall be separated from her husband by their mutual consent, and after his ordination and consecration to the episcopate she shall enter a monastery situated at a distance from the abode of the bishop, and there let her enjoy the bishop's provision. And if she is deemed worthy, she may be advanced to the dignity of a deaconess (Sixth Ecumenical Council, canon 48).[47]

9. *Ecclesiastical blessing legally required*

Ancient custom was rather indifferently disposed towards adoption of children and considered that there was nothing wrong in it taking place without prayers and sacramental action. It also failed to impose any rigorous formality in connection with marriage and permitted it to happen without blessing. But even if a reason can be found, explaining this state of affairs in ancient times, there is no reason why we should neglect either one of these two institutions, since, by the grace of God, we have reached a higher and holier level of social life.

We have therefore prescribed that adoption of children should take place with holy invocations (novella 24). We now also order that marriages be confirmed with a sacred blessing, and if the couple will neglect

---

[47]We have discussed above the historical reasons which explain why the Church, in the sixth and seventh centuries, ceased to allow married men to the episcopate. The present canon, which seems to contradict the principle of indissolubility of marriage, so clearly stated elsewhere, is very rarely applied.

that procedure, their cohabitation will not be considered at any time as marriage, and will not produce the legal effects of marriage. For, apart from celibacy and marriage, there is no other irreproachable situation. Do you desire to marry? You must observe the laws of marriage. You do not like to marry? Then practice celibacy, but do not adulterate marriage and do not make pretence of celibacy (Emperor Leo VI [886-912], novella 89, issued before the emperor's own third and fourth marriages).

The Liturgical Tradition

Marriage and Holy Communion
According to St. Symeon of Thessalonica
(d. 1420)

St. Symeon, archbishop of Thessalonica, is the author of a well known commentary on the various services and sacraments of the Church as they were celebrated in his time. After describing the rite of crowning, the prayers said by the priest, and the saying together of the Lord's prayer, St. Symeon continues:

> And immediately (the priest), takes the holy chalice with the Presanctified Gifts, and exclaims: "The Presanctified holy Things for the Holy." And all respond: "One is Holy, One is Lord," because the Lord alone is the sanctification, the peace and the union of His servants who are being married. The priest then gives Communion to the bridal pair, if they are worthy. Indeed, they must be ready to receive Communion, so that their crowning be a worthy one and their marriage valid. For Holy Communion is the perfection of every sacrament and the seal of every mystery. And the Church is right in preparing the Divine Gifts for the redemption and blessing of the bridal pair; for Christ Himself, Who gave us these Gifts and Who is the Gifts, came to the marriage (in Cana of Galilee) to

bring to it peaceful union and control. So that those who get married must be worthy of Holy Communion; they must be united before God in a church, which is the house of God, because they are children of God, in a church where God is sacramentally present in the Gifts, where He is being offered to us and where He is seen in the midst of us.

After that the priest also gives them to drink from the common cup; and the hymn "I will receive the cup of salvation," is sung because of the Most Holy Gifts, and as a sign of the joy which comes from divine union, and because the joy of the bridal pair comes from the peace and concord which they have received.

But to those who are not worthy of Communion—for example those who are being married a second time, and others—the Divine Gifts are not given, but only the common cup, as a partial sanctification, as a sign of good fellowship and unity with God's blessing. (*Against the Heresies and on the Divine Temple,* Chap. 282, PG 155, col. 512-513.)

The Marriage Service

THE SERVICE OF BETROTHAL

The betrothal is celebrated in the narthex, or in the back part of the church.

DEACON: Bless, Master.

PRIEST: Blessed is our God, always, now and ever and unto ages of ages.

CHOIR: Amen.

DEACON: In peace let us pray to the Lord.

CHOIR: Lord, have mercy. (*Repeated after each petition.*) For the peace from above and for the salvation of our souls, let us pray to the Lord.

For the peace of the whole world, for the welfare of the holy churches of God, and for the union of all, let us pray to the Lord.

For this holy house and for those who enter with faith, reverence, and the fear of God, let us pray to the Lord.

For our Metropolitan ——————, for our Bishop ——————, for the honorable priesthood, the diaconate in Christ, for all the clergy and the people, let us pray to the Lord.

For the servant of God ——————, and for the handmaiden of God ——————, who now plight each other their troth, and for their salvation, let us pray to the Lord.

That they may be granted children for the continuation of the race, and all their petitions which are unto salvation, let us pray to the Lord.

That He will send down upon them perfect and peaceful love, and assistance, let us pray to the Lord.

That He will preserve them in oneness of mind, and in steadfast faith, let us pray to the Lord.

That He will preserve them in a blameless way of life, let us pray to the Lord.

That the Lord our God will grant to them an honorable marriage and a bed undefiled, let us pray to the Lord.

For our deliverance from all affliction, wrath, danger, and necessity, let us pray to the Lord.

Help us, save us, have mercy on us, and keep us, O God, by Thy grace.

CHOIR: Lord, have mercy.

DEACON: Commemorating our most holy, most pure, most blessed and glorious Lady Theotokos and ever-virgin Mary, with all the saints, let us commend ourselves and each other, and all our life unto Christ our God.

CHOIR: To Thee, O Lord.

PRIEST: For unto Thee are due all glory, honor and worship: to the Father, and to the Son, and to the Holy Spirit, now and ever and unto ages of ages.

CHOIR: Amen.

PRIEST: O eternal God, who hast brought into unity those
          who were sundered, and hast ordained for them
          an indissoluble bond of love, who didst bless Isaac
          and Rebecca, and didst make them heirs of Thy
          promise: Bless also these Thy servants, ————
          and ————, guiding them unto every good
          work. For Thou art a good God and lovest man-
          kind, and unto Thee we ascribe glory: to the
          Father, and to the Son, and to the Holy Spirit,
          now and ever and unto ages of ages.

CHOIR: Amen.

PRIEST: Peace be unto all.

CHOIR: And to your spirit.

DEACON: Bow your heads unto the Lord.

CHOIR: To Thee, O Lord.

PRIEST: O Lord our God, who hast espoused the Church
          as a pure virgin from among the gentiles: Bless
          this betrothal, and unite and maintain these Thy
          servants in peace and oneness of mind. For unto
          Thee are due all glory, honor, and worship: to the
          Father, and to the Son, and to the Holy Spirit, now
          and ever and unto ages of ages.

CHOIR: Amen.

*Then taking the rings, the priest blesses the bridal pair,
making the sign of the cross with the ring of the bride over
the bridegroom, and with that of the bridegroom over the
bride, saying to the man*: The servant of God, ————, is
          betrothed to the handmaiden of God, ————, in
          the name of the Father, and of the Son, and of
          the Holy Spirit. Amen.

And to the woman: The handmaiden of God, ————,
          is betrothed to the servant of God, ————,
          in the name of the Father, and of the Son, and
          of the Holy Spirit. Amen.

And when he has said this to each of them three times, he places the rings on their right hands. Then the bridal pair exchanges the rings, and the priest says the following prayer:

DEACON: Let us pray to the Lord.

CHOIR: Lord, have mercy.

PRIEST: O Lord our God, who didst accompany the servant of the patriarch Abraham into Mesopotamia, when he was sent to espouse a wife for his lord Isaac, and who, by means of the drawing of water, didst reveal to him that he should betroth Rebecca: Do Thou, the same Lord, bless also the betrothal of these Thy servants, _____ and _____, and confirm the promise that they have made. Establish them in the holy union which is from Thee. For in the beginning Thou didst make them male and female, and by Thee the woman is joined unto the man as a helper and for the procreation of the human race. Therefore, O Lord our God, who hast sent forth Thy truth upon Thine inheritance, and Thy covenant unto Thy servants our fathers, Thine elect from generation to generation: Look upon Thy servant, _____, and thy handmaiden, _____, and establish and make firm their betrothal, in faith and in oneness of mind, in truth and in love. For Thou, O Lord, hast declared that a pledge should be given and confirmed in all things. By a ring power was given to Joseph in Egypt; by a ring Daniel was glorified in the land of Babylon; by a ring the uprightness of Tamar was revealed; by a ring our heavenly Father showed His bounty upon His Son, for He said: Bring the fatted calf and kill it, and let us eat and make merry. By Thine own right hand, O Lord, Thou didst arm Moses in the Red Sea; by Thy true word the heavens were established, and the foundations of the earth were made firm; and the right hands of Thy servants also shall be blessed by Thy mighty word and by Thine upraised arm. Therefore, O Master, bless now this putting-on of rings with Thy heavenly blessing, and let Thine angel go before them all the days of their life. For Thou art He that blesses and sanctifies all things, and unto Thee are due all glory, honor, and worship: to the Father, and to the Son, and to the Holy Spirit, now and ever and unto ages of ages.

CHOIR: Amen.

THE SERVICE OF CROWNING

The bridal couple, preceded by the Priest, moves in procession to the center of the church.

PRIEST AND CHOIR. *Refrain*: Glory to Thee, our God, glory to Thee!

Blessed is every one who fears the Lord, who walks in his ways!

You shall eat the fruit of the labor of your hands; you shall be happy, and it shall be well with you.

Your wife will be like a fruitful vine within your house;

your children will be like olive shoots around your table.

Lo, thus shall the man be blessed who fears the Lord.

The Lord bless you from Zion!

May you see the prosperity of Jerusalem all the days of your life!

May you see your children's children!

Peace be upon Israel!   (Ps. 128)

[*An exhortation may follow. Then, according to Slavonic editions of the marriage service, the priest shall inquire of the bridegroom*: Do you, —————, have a good, free and unconstrained will and a firm intention to take as your wife this woman, —————, whom you see here before you?

BRIDEGROOM: I have, reverend father.

PRIEST: Have you promised yourself to any other bride?

BRIDEGROOM: I have not promised myself, reverend father.

And the priest, looking at the bride, shall inquire of her: Do you, —————, have a good, free and unconstrained will and a firm intention to take as your husband this man, —————, whom you see here before you?

BRIDE: I have, reverend father.

PRIEST: Have you promised yourself to any other man?

BRIDE: I have not promised myself, reverend father.]

DEACON: Bless, master.

PRIEST: Blessed is the Kingdom of the Father, and of the Son, and of the Holy Spirit, now and ever and unto ages of ages.

CHOIR: Amen.

DEACON: In peace let us pray to the Lord.

CHOIR: Lord, have mercy. (*Repeated after each petition.*)

For the peace from above and for the salvation of our souls, let us pray to the Lord.

For the peace of the whole world, for the welfare of the holy churches of God, and for the union of all, let us pray to the Lord.

For this holy house and for those who enter with faith, reverence, and the fear of God, let us pray to the Lord.

For our Metropolitan ————, for our Bishop ————, for the honorable priesthood, the diaconate in Christ, for all the clergy and the people, let us pray to the Lord.

For the servants of God, ———— and ————, who are now being united to each other in the community of marriage, and for their salvation, let us pray to the Lord.

That He will bless this marriage, as He blessed the marriage in Cana of Galilee, let us pray to the Lord.

That He will grant to them chastity, and of the fruit of the womb as is expedient for them, let us pray to the Lord.

That He will make them glad with the sight of sons and daughters, let us pray to the Lord.

That He will grant to them enjoyment of the blessing of children, and a blameless life, let us pray to the Lord.

That He will grant to them and to us, all our petitions which are unto salvation, let us pray to the Lord.

That He will deliver them and us from all affliction, wrath, danger, and necessity, let us pray to the Lord.

Help us, save us, have mercy on us, and keep us, O God, by Thy grace.

CHOIR: Lord, have mercy.

DEACON: Commemorating our most holy, most pure, most blessed and glorious Lady Theotokos and ever-virgin Mary, with all the saints, let us commend ourselves and each other, and all our life unto Christ our God.

CHOIR: To Thee, O Lord.

PRIEST: For unto Thee are due all glory, honor, and worship: to the Father, and to the Son, and to the Holy
Spirit, now and ever and unto ages of ages.

CHOIR: Amen.

DEACON: Let us pray to the Lord.

CHOIR: Lord, have mercy.

Then the priest recites aloud the following prayer: O God
most pure, fashioner of every creature, who didst
transform the rib of our forefather Adam into a
wife, because of Thy love towards mankind, and
didst bless them and say to them: Be fruitful and
multiply, and fill the earth and subdue it; who
didst make of the two one flesh: Therefore a man
leaves his father and his mother and cleaves to
his wife, and the two shall become one flesh, and
what God has joined together, let no man put
asunder: Thou didst bless Thy servant Abraham,
and opening the womb of Sarah didst make him
to be the father of many nations. Thou didst give
Isaac to Rebecca, and didst bless her in childbearing. Thou didst join Jacob unto Rachel, and
from them didst bring forth the twelve patriarchs.
Thou didst unite Joseph and Aseneth, giving to
them Ephraim and Manasseh as the fruit of their
procreation. Thou didst accept Zechariah and
Elizabeth, and didst make their offspring to be the
Forerunner. From the root of Jesse according to
the flesh, Thou didst bud forth the ever-virgin
one, and wast incarnate of her, and wast born of
her for the redemption of the human race. Through
Thine unutterable gift and manifold goodness,
Thou didst come to Cana of Galilee, and didst
bless the marriage there, to make manifest that it
is Thy will that there should be lawful marriage
and procreation. Do Thou, the same all-holy
Master, accept the prayers of us Thy servants.
As Thou wast present there, be Thou also present

here, with Thine invisible protection. Bless this marriage, and grant to these Thy servants, ——————— and ———————, a peaceful life, length of days, chastity, mutual love in the bond of peace, long-lived offspring, gratitude from their children, a crown of glory that does not fade away. Graciously grant that they may see their children's children. Preserve their bed unassailed, and give them of the dew of heaven from on high, and of the fatness of the earth. Fill their houses with wheat, wine and oil and with every good thing, so that they may give in turn to those in need; and grant also to those here present with them all those petitions which are for their salvation. For Thou art the God of mercies, and of bounties, and love towards mankind, and unto Thee we ascribe glory: to the Father, and to the Son, and to the Holy Spirit, now and ever and unto ages of ages.

CHOIR: Amen.

DEACON: Let us pray to the Lord.

CHOIR: Lord, have mercy.

Then the priest recites aloud the following prayer: Blessed art Thou, O Lord our God, priest of mystical and undefiled marriage, and ordainer of the law of the marriage of the body; preserver of immortality, and provider of the good things of life; the same master who in the beginning didst make man and establish him as a king over creation, and didst say: "It is not good that man should be alone upon the earth. Let us make a helper fit for him." Taking one of his ribs, Thou didst fashion woman; and when Adam saw her he said: "This is at last bone of my bones and flesh of my flesh; she shall be called Woman, because she was taken out of Man." For this reason a man shall leave his father and mother and be joined to his wife,

and the two shall become one flesh; what therefore God has joined together, let no man put
asunder: Do Thou now also, O Master, our Lord
and our God, send down Thy heavenly grace upon
these Thy servants, _____ and _____;
grant that this Thy handmaiden may be subject to
her husband in all things, and that this Thy
servant may be the head of his wife, so that they
may live according to Thy will. Bless them,
O Lord our God, as Thou didst bless Abraham
and Sarah. Bless them, O Lord our God, as Thou
didst bless Isaac and Rebecca. Bless them, O Lord
our God, as Thou didst bless Jacob and all the
patriarchs. Bless them, O Lord our God, as Thou
didst bless Joseph and Aseneth. Bless them, O Lord
our God, as Thou didst bless Moses and Zipporah.
Bless them, O Lord our God, as Thou didst bless
Joachim and Anna. Bless them, O Lord our God,
as Thou didst bless Zechariah and Elizabeth. Preserve them, O Lord our God, as Thou didst preserve Noah in the ark. Preserve them, O Lord
our God, as Thou didst preserve Jonah in the belly
of the whale. Preserve them, O Lord our God, as
Thou didst preserve the three holy children from
the fire, sending down upon them dew from
heaven; and let that gladness come upon them
which the blessed Helen had when she found the
precious cross. Remember them, O Lord our God,
as Thou didst remember Enoch, Shem, Elijah.
Remember them, O Lord our God, as Thou didst
remember Thy forty holy martyrs, sending down
upon them crowns from heaven. Remember them,
O Lord our God, and the parents who have nur-
tured them, for the prayers of parents make firm
the foundations of houses. Remember, O Lord
our God, Thy servants the groomsman and the
bridesmaid of the bridal pair, who have come
together in this joy. Remember, O Lord our God,
Thy servant, _____, and Thy handmaiden,

————————, and bless them. Grant them of the fruit of their bodies, fair children, concord of soul and body. Exalt them like the cedars of Lebanon, like a luxuriant vine. Give them offspring in number like unto full ears of grain; so that, having enough of all things, they may abound in every work that is good and acceptable unto Thee. Let them see their children's children, like olive shoots around their table; so that, finding favor in Thy sight, they may shine like the stars of heaven, in Thee our God. For unto Thee are due all glory, honor, and worship: to the Father, and to the Son, and to the Holy Spirit, now and ever and unto ages of ages.

CHOIR: Amen.

DEACON: Let us pray to the Lord.

CHOIR: Lord, have mercy.

And again the priest prays aloud: O holy God, who didst form man from the dust, and didst fashion woman from his rib, and didst join her unto him as a helper, for it seemed good to Thy majesty that man should not be alone upon the earth: Do Thou, the same Lord, stretch out now also Thy hand from Thy holy dwelling-place, and unite this Thy servant, ————————, and this Thy handmaiden, ————————; for by Thee is the husband joined unto the wife. Unite them in one mind; wed them into one flesh, granting to them the fruit of the body and the procreation of fair children. For Thine is the majesty, and Thine is the Kingdom and the power and the glory: of the Father, and of the Son, and of the Holy Spirit, now and ever and unto ages of ages.

CHOIR: Amen.

The priest takes the crowns, which recall those with which the "martyrs," or witnesses of Christ, are crowned in heaven,

and crowns first the bridegroom, saying: The servant of
God, ————, is crowned unto the handmaiden
of God, ————: in the name of the Father,
and of the Son, and of the Holy Spirit.

So also he crowns the bride, saying: The handmaiden of God,
————, is crowned unto the servant of God,
————: in the name of the Father, and of the
Son, and of the Holy Spirit.

Then he blesses them three times, saying each time: O Lord
our God, crown them with glory and honor.

DEACON: Let us attend.

PRIEST: Peace be unto all.

READER: And to your spirit.

DEACON: Wisdom!

READER: The prokeimenon in the eighth tone (Ps. 21):
Thou hast set upon their heads crowns of precious
stones; they asked life of Thee, and Thou gavest
it them.

VERSE: Yea, Thou wilt make them most blessed for ever;
Thou wilt make them glad with the joy of Thy
presence.

DEACON: Wisdom!

READER: The reading is from the Epistle of the holy Apostle
Paul to the Ephesians.

DEACON: Let us attend.

READER: (Eph. 5:20-33) Brethren: Give thanks always and
for everything in the name of our Lord Jesus Christ
to God the Father. Be subject to one another out
of reverence for Christ. Wives, be subject to your
husbands, as to the Lord. For the husband is the
head of the wife as Christ is the head of the church,
His body, and is Himself its Savior. As the church
is subject to Christ, so let wives also be subject in

everything to their husbands. Husbands, love your wives, as Christ loved the church and gave Himself up for her, that He might sanctify her, having cleansed her by the washing of water with the word, that the church might be presented before Him in splendor, without spot or wrinkle or any such thing, that she might be holy and without blemish. Even so husbands should love their wives as their own bodies. He who loves his wife loves himself. For no man ever hates his own flesh, but nourishes and cherishes it, as Christ does the church, because we are members of His body. "For this reason a man shall leave his father and mother and be joined to his wife, and the two shall become one." This is a great mystery, and I take it to mean Christ and the church; however, let each one of you love his wife as himself and let the wife see that she respects her husband.

PRIEST: Peace be unto you, reader.

READER: And to your spirit. Alleluia! Alleluia! Alleluia!

VERSE: (Ps. 12; tone 5): Thou, O Lord, shalt protect us and preserve us from this generation forever.

PRIEST: Peace be unto all.

CHOIR: And to your spirit.

PRIEST: The reading is from the Holy Gospel according to Saint John.

CHOIR: Glory to Thee, O Lord, glory to Thee.

DEACON: Let us attend.

PRIEST: (John 2:1-11) In those days there was a marriage at Cana in Galilee, and the mother of Jesus was there; Jesus also was invited to the marriage, with His disciples. When the wine failed, the mother of Jesus said to Him, "They have no wine." And Jesus said to her, "O woman, what have you to do with me? My hour has not yet come." His

mother said to the servants, "Do whatever He
tells you." Now six stone jars were standing there,
for the Jewish rites of purification, each holding
twenty or thirty gallons. Jesus said to them, "Fill
the jars with water." And they filled them up to
the brim. He said to them, "Now draw some out,
and take it to the steward of the feast." So they
took it. When the steward of the feast tasted the
water now become wine, and did not know where
it came from (though the servants who had drawn
the water knew), the steward of the feast called
the bridegroom and said to him, "Every man serves
the good wine first; and when men have drunk
freely, then the poor wine; but you have kept the
good wine until now." This, the first of his signs,
Jesus did at Cana in Galilee, and manifested His
glory; and His disciples believed in Him.

CHOIR: Glory to Thee, O Lord, glory to Thee.

DEACON: Let us all say with all our soul and with all our
mind, let us say.

CHOIR: Lord, have mercy.

DEACON: O Lord almighty, the God of our Fathers, we pray
Thee, hearken and have mercy.

CHOIR: Lord, have mercy.

DEACON: Have mercy on us, O God, according to Thy great
goodness, we pray Thee, hearken and have mercy.

CHOIR: Lord, have mercy. (3)

DEACON: Again we pray for mercy, life, peace, health, salvation, and visitation for the servants of God,
_____ and _____ (*and he mentions also
whomever else he wishes*), and for the pardon
and remission of their sins.

CHOIR: Lord, have mercy. (3)

PRIEST: For Thou art a merciful God, and lovest mankind,

and unto Thee we ascribe glory: to the Father, and to the Son, and to the Holy Spirit, now and ever and unto ages of ages.

CHOIR: Amen.

DEACON: Let us pray to the Lord.

CHOIR: Lord, have mercy.

PRIEST: O Lord our God, who in Thy saving dispensation didst vouchsafe by Thy presence in Cana of Galilee to declare marriage honorable: Do Thou, the same Lord, now also maintain in peace and concord Thy servants, ———— and ————, whom Thou hast been pleased to join together. Cause their marriage to be honorable. Preserve their bed blameless. Mercifully grant that they may live together in purity; and enable them to reach a ripe old age, walking in Thy commandments with a pure heart. For Thou art our God, the God of mercy and salvation, and unto Thee we ascribe glory: to the Father, and to the Son, and to the Holy Spirit, now and ever and unto ages of ages.

CHOIR: Amen.

DEACON: Help us, save us, have mercy on us, and keep us, O God, by Thy grace.

CHOIR: Lord, have mercy.

DEACON: That the whole day may be perfect, holy, peaceful, and sinless, let us ask of the Lord.

CHOIR: Grant it, O Lord. (*Repeated after each petition.*)

An angel of peace, a faithful guide, a guardian of our souls and bodies, let us ask of the Lord.

Pardon and remission of our sins and transgressions, let us ask of the Lord.

All things that are good and profitable for our souls, and peace for the world, let us ask of the Lord.

That we may complete the remaining time of our life in peace and repentance, let us ask of the Lord.

A Christian ending to our life: painless, blameless, and peaceful; and a good defense before the dread judgment seat of Christ, let us ask of the Lord.

CHOIR: Grant it, O Lord.

DEACON: Having asked for the unity of the Faith, and the communion of the Holy Spirit, let us commend ourselves and each other, and all our life unto Christ our God.

CHOIR: To Thee, O Lord.

PRIEST: And make us worthy, O Master, that with boldness and without condemnation we may dare to call on Thee, the heavenly God, as Father, and to say:

CHOIR: Our Father, who art in heaven, hallowed be Thy name. Thy Kingdom come. Thy will be done, on earth as it is in heaven. Give us this day our daily bread; and forgive us our trespasses, as we forgive those who trespass against us; and lead us not into temptation, but deliver us from evil.

PRIEST: For Thine is the Kingdom, and the power, and the glory: of the Father, and of the Son, and of the Holy Spirit, now and ever and unto ages of ages.

CHOIR: Amen.

PRIEST: Peace be unto all.

CHOIR: And to your spirit.

DEACON: Bow your heads unto the Lord.

CHOIR: To Thee, O Lord.

Then the common cup is brought and the priest blesses it.

DEACON: Let us pray to the Lord.

CHOIR: Lord, have mercy.

PRIEST: O God, who hast created all things by Thy might, and hast made firm the world, and adornest the crown of all that Thou hast made: Bless now, with Thy spiritual blessing, this common cup, which Thou dost give to those who are now united for the community of marriage. For blessed is Thy name, and glorified is Thy Kingdom, of the Father, and of the Son, and of the Holy Spirit, now and ever and unto ages of ages.

CHOIR: Amen.

Then, taking the cup, the priest gives it to them three times: first to the bridegroom and then to the bride. Then immediately the priest takes them, the groomsmen behind them holding their crowns, and leads them in a circle three times around the lectern. And the priest or the choir sings:

Rejoice, O Isaiah! A virgin is with child; and shall bear a Son, Emmanuel. He is both God and man; and Orient is His name. Magnifying Him, we call the virgin blessed.

O holy martyrs, who fought the good fight and have received your crowns: Entreat ye the Lord, that He will have mercy on our souls.

Glory to Thee, O Christ God, the apostles' boast, the martyrs' joy, whose preaching was the consubstantial Trinity.

Then, taking the crown of the bridegroom, the priest says:
Be exalted like Abraham, O Bridegroom, and be blessed like Isaac, and multiply like Jacob, walking in peace, and keeping God's commandments in righteousness.

Then, taking the crown of the bride, he says: And you, O bride: Be exalted like Sarah, and exult like Rebecca, and multiply like Rachel; and rejoice in your husband, fulfilling the conditions of the law, for this is well-pleasing to God.

DEACON: Let us pray to the Lord.

CHOIR: Lord, have mercy.

PRIEST: O God, our God, who didst come to Cana of Galilee, and didst bless there the marriage feast: Bless also these Thy servants, who through Thy good providence now are united in wedlock. Bless their goings out and their comings in. Fill their life with good things. Receive their crowns into Thy Kingdom, preserving them spotless, blameless, and without reproach, unto ages of ages.

CHOIR: Amen.

PRIEST: Peace be unto all.

CHOIR: And to your spirit.

DEACON: Bow your heads unto the Lord.

CHOIR: To Thee, O Lord.

PRIEST: May the Father, and the Son, and the Holy Spirit, the all-holy, consubstantial, and life-giving Trinity, one Godhead and one Kingdom, bless you; and grant you length of days, fair children, progress in life and faith; and fill you with all earthly good things, and make you worthy to enjoy the good things of the promise; through the prayers of the holy Theotokos and of all saints. Amen.

DEACON: Most holy Theotokos, save us!

CHOIR: More honorable than the Cherubim, and more glorious beyond compare than the Seraphim: without defilement you gave birth to God the Word: true Theotokos, we magnify you.

PRIEST: Glory to Thee, O Christ our God and our hope, glory to Thee.

CHOIR: Glory to the Father, and to the Son, and to the Holy Spirit, now and ever and unto ages of ages. Amen. Lord have mercy. (3) Father, bless.

PRIEST: May He who by His presence in Cana of Galilee declared marriage to be honorable, Christ our true God, through the prayers of His most pure mother; of the holy, glorious, and all-laudable apostles; of the holy, God-crowned kings Constantine and Helen, equal to the apostles; of the holy great martyr Procopius; and of all the saints: have mercy on us and save us, for He is good and loves mankind.

CHOIR: Amen.